First World War

and Army of Occupation

War Diary

France, Belgium and Germany

28 DIVISION
Divisional Troops
Royal Army Medical Corps
85 Field Ambulance
1 January 1915 - 31 October 1915

WO95/2272/6

The Naval & Military Press Ltd
www.nmarchive.com
Published in association with The National Archives

Published by

The Naval & Military Press Ltd

Unit 10 Ridgewood Industrial Park,

Uckfield, East Sussex,

TN22 5QE England

Tel: +44 (0) 1825 749494

www.naval-military-press.com

www.nmarchive.com

This diary has been reprinted in facsimile from the original. Any imperfections are inevitably reproduced and the quality may fall short of modern type and cartographic standards.

Contents

Document type	Place/Title	Date From	Date To
Heading	WO95/2272/6		
Heading	28th Division Medical 85th Fld Ambulance Jan-Oct 1915		
Heading	121/4538 Jan 1915 85th Field Ambulance Vol I		
War Diary	Hursley Winchester	01/01/1915	01/01/1915
War Diary	Hursley Winchester	02/01/1915	31/01/1915
Heading	121/4538 Feb 1915 85 Field Ambulance Vol II		
War Diary		01/02/1915	28/02/1915
Heading	121/5113 March 1915 85th Field Ambulance Vol III		
War Diary		01/03/1915	30/03/1915
Miscellaneous	Classification Of Wounded Appendix II		
Miscellaneous	Report On Interview With D.M.S. Of 9th French Army Corps relative to Bad Feet	12/02/1915	12/02/1915
Heading	28th Division 121/6243 85th Field Ambulance Vol IV April 15		
War Diary		01/04/1915	30/04/1915
Miscellaneous	Classification of Wounded Appendix II		
Heading	April 1915		
Miscellaneous	Appendix I	09/04/1915	09/04/1915
Heading	28th Division 121/6243 85th Field Ambulance Vol V May 15		
War Diary		01/05/1915	31/05/1915
Miscellaneous	Classification of Wounded Appendix I		
Heading	No 85. F.A. May 1915		
Heading	28th Division 121/6243 85th Field Ambulance Vol VI June 15		
War Diary		01/06/1915	30/06/1915
Heading	28th Division 121/6243 85th Field Ambulance Vol VII July 15		
War Diary		01/07/1915	31/07/1915
Miscellaneous	Classification of Wounded Appendix I		
Heading	28th Division 85th Field Ambulance Vol VIII August 15		
War Diary		01/08/1915	31/08/1915
Miscellaneous	Classification of Wounded Appendix I		
Miscellaneous	Classification of Wounded		
Heading	28th Division 85th Field Ambulance Vol IX Sept 15		
War Diary		01/09/1915	30/09/1915
Miscellaneous	Classification of Wounded Appendix I		
Map	Appendix II		
Heading	28th Division 85th Field Ambulance Vol X Oct 15		
War Diary		01/10/1915	31/10/1915
Miscellaneous	Classification of Wounded Appendix I		

WO 95/2272 (6)

28TH DIVISION
MEDICAL

85TH FLD AMBULANCE

JAN - OCT 1915

121/4538
Jan 1915

85th Field Ambulance

Vol I.

Instructions regarding War Diaries and Intelligence Summaries are contained in F. S. Regs., Part II. and the Staff Manual respectively. Title pages will be prepared in manuscript.

WAR DIARY
or
INTELLIGENCE SUMMARY
(Erase heading not required.)

85 F Amb

Army Form C. 2118.

Hour, Date, Place	Summary of Events and Information	Remarks and references to Appendices
1915 Hursley, Winchester	Sent away 6 Horses with mange –	
Jan 1st	Inoculated men of 2/Cheshires	
	Started course of Instruction for Stretcher Bearers (Regimental) & water duty men & Sanitary Squads of Battalions.	
HURSLEY	50% of Personnel went on leave (2 days)	
	Admissions to F.A. = 7. Malaria & Rheumatism	
2nd	By order of A.D.M.S. went up to War Office to clear up uncertainty as to whether our own or Bristol ambulances would accompany us to front:	
	Lt. Major Wapple in command	
	Saw Major Foster DDMS at War Office who wired to A.D.M.S. confirming arrangement that we should take our own of Bristol Ambulances. Admitted to F.A. 6.	
3rd	Conditions in camp being very bad. 2 Battalions of 84th Brigade ordered into billets in WINCHESTER also the 3rd London Field Ambulance. We were ordered to leave all horses, harness & [illegible] with the [illegible] Admitted to F.A. = 4.	
5th	Drew from ordnance 7 limbered wagons, some harness, [illegible]	
	The ARBOR was allotted to us for horse lines –	

Instructions regarding War Diaries and Intelligence Summaries are contained in F. S. Regs., Part II. and the Staff Manual respectively. Title pages will be prepared in manuscript.

WAR DIARY
or
INTELLIGENCE SUMMARY

(Erase heading not required.)

Army Form C. 2118.

Hour, Date, Place	Summary of Events and Information	Remarks and references to Appendices
	Ordered to move into billets at "West Downs" School & Pinebank House & open H. for 80 Beds.	
	B Section opened a 20 bed H. in Pinebank House & A + C Sections a 60 bed H. in West Downs.	
Jan 6th	Drew 4 mules & 39 horses from Remount Depot & about ½ our Ordnance Equipment. Transport occupied in assembling & fitting harness. Admitted to H: 7.	
7th	Remainder of horses up to [illegible] – drew 50% of [illegible] clothing. Admitted to H = 6	
8th	Returned all old equipment to Woolwich & old clothing to Devonport & [illegible] Equipment to Reserve Unit. Drew 3 Ambulance wagons & 2 water carts. Admitted H: 7	
9th	Completed wheeled transport & harness	
10th	Having transport vehicles painted with Red + [illegible]. Completed harness fitting & drew balance of unit's Stores & Equipment. Took unit for Route March with transport, no difficulties except such as were due to [illegible] want of Medical Store wagon for a pair of horses. –	

1247 W 3299 200,000 (E) 8/14 J.B.C. & A. Forms/C. 2118/11.

3/

Instructions regarding War Diaries and Intelligence Summaries are contained in F. S. Regs., Part II. and the Staff Manual respectively. Title pages will be prepared in manuscript.

WAR DIARY
or
INTELLIGENCE SUMMARY
(Erase heading not required.)

Army Form C. 2118.

Hour, Date, Place	Summary of Events and Information	Remarks and references to Appendices
Jan 15th	Cleared up all old Corps & Coy offices & sent all old papers to base depot. Received orders to embark tomorrow. Completed personnel & reinforcements from Reserve.	
16th	Paraded at 6-20 am packed wagons, cleared up billets. Entrained outside 'West Downs' at 9.20 am. at Southampton 2.30. Embarked personnel & horses in 'Kingstonian' & vehicles in 'Australind'. Left dock at 6.20 pm. Paraded men on deck when clear of dock & read the King's message to the troops & distributed copies to the men. Anchored in Southampton water for night. The vehicles containing equipment being on another vessel. [illegible] have been very awkward if any [illegible] had occurred during the passage. On board besides 3rd London Field Ambulance were HQ 31st Brigade RFA & 1 Battery & 1 Squadron [illegible]	
17th	Calm night. Church Parade at 10.30. Sailed at 12.30 pm. Good passage	

W 3999 200,000 (E) 8/14 J.B.C. & A. Forms/C. 2118/13.

34

Instructions regarding War Diaries and Intelligence Summaries are contained in F. S. Regs., Part II. and the Staff Manual respectively. Title pages will be prepared in manuscript.

WAR DIARY

or

INTELLIGENCE SUMMARY

(Erase heading not required.)

Army Form C. 2118.

Hour, Date, Place	Summary of Events and Information	Remarks and references to Appendices
Jan 18th	Landed at ~~Havre~~ HAVRE 1 pm. – Just before landing discovered Pte A. Wood of this unit to be suffering from Scarlet Fever. & 1 other man of mine & 2 of Surrey Yeomanry to have tonsillitis. Got on phone to A.D.M.S. who ordered all to be sent to No 2 General Hospital & 2 contacts to be isolated. Left latter at No 1 Camp. [illegible] reported to him as Interpreter. [illegible] disembarked & drew [illegible] wagons for MT. [illegible] & marched to No 2 Camp for drivers. Rations [illegible] the night. Received orders to entrain at 5.30 pm 19th	
19th	Paraded 3-15 pm – & marched to Point 3. arrived 4.20 pm. Loaded wagons – all side loading & very awkward & tedious process. Train Started at 9.25 pm. ~~for~~ Rouen – Darnetal. Abbeville. Etaples. Boulogne. Calais	
20th	St Omer. Hazebrouck. arrived 8.20 pm. 20th Reinforcement was left at No 1 Rest Camp HAVRE. Went into billets for the night.	
~~21st~~	The driving of the train was atrocious. frequent severe shocks throwing horses off their legs. Train of 50 trucks. too long. Train also carried draft of "Kings Own" & 1 company A.S.C.	
21st	Paraded at 9 am. & marched to STRAZEELE. where we went into billets & established HP in School. [illegible] 16 sick from the Brigade.	

1247 W 3299 200,000 (E) 8/14 J.B.C. & A. Forms/C. 2118/11.

5

Instructions regarding War Diaries and Intelligence Summaries are contained in F. S. Regs., Part II. and the Staff Manual respectively. Title pages will be prepared in manuscript.

WAR DIARY
or
INTELLIGENCE SUMMARY

(Erase heading not required.)

Army Form C. 2118.

Hour, Date, Place	Summary of Events and Information	Remarks and references to Appendices
Jan 22nd	Settled into billets - H.Q. - admitted 15 sick. including Captain HOBBS. 1st Welsh. & Col: ALLEN. the A.D.M.S. 28th Division.	
23rd	Admitted 26 sick & transferred to Clearing H. 20. 1 case Scarlet fever in unit transferred with 3 contacts to HAZEBROUCKE. Water supply not reliable. Therefore chlorinated all water used for drinking. Route march - M.S. wagon also proved to be heavily laden for a pair in these very bad roads - heavy line train heard beyond BALLIEUL.	
24th	Billets of the Brigade not sanitary. Detailed Capt. R.E. Potter to act as Sanitary Officer for the Brigade & Divisional H.Q. Guard areas. Engaged all day in making billets more sanitary & getting units to dig trench latrines. [illegible] Admitted 19 sick & transferred 15 to Clearing Hospl. Admitted Major SCOTT 2/Cheshire & Lieut FORREST A.V.C.	

6

Instructions regarding War Diaries and Intelligence Summaries are contained in F. S. Regs., Part II. and the Staff Manual respectively. Title pages will be prepared in manuscript.

WAR DIARY
or
INTELLIGENCE SUMMARY

(Erase heading not required.)

Army Form C. 2118.

Hour, Date, Place	Summary of Events and Information	Remarks and references to Appendices
Jan 26th	Admitted 27. Transferred 27. Illness mainly Bronchitis, Influenza, Tonsillitis. Route march 9.30 till 1 o/c.	
28th	Brigade inspected by General Sir J. French. Admitted 15 including Lieut LEACH 1/Suffolks. ~~Discharged~~ 17. Transferred. Made water supply [illegible] of annex ward	
29th	Admitted 5. Transferred 5. Discharged 3. Visit of Lt/Col. Ferguson our new A.D.M.S. to whom I gave a report of the unit. Route march to inspect practice trenches at [illegible] & to locate position for Dressing Station La Couronne	
30th	Admitted 15. Transferred 3.	
31st	Admitted 10. Transferred 8. Discharged 2. Major Clements reported his arrival, to be attached to the unit for instructional purposes for 10 days or a fortnight.	[illegible signature]

121/4538
Feb 1915

85 Field Ambulance

Vol II

85 F Amb

Army Form C. 2118.

WAR DIARY
or
INTELLIGENCE SUMMARY

(Erase heading not required.)

Instructions regarding War Diaries and Intelligence Summaries are contained in F. S. Regs., Part II. and the Staff Manual respectively. Title pages will be prepared in manuscript.

Hour, Date, Place	Summary of Events and Information	Remarks and references to Appendices
1915 February 1st	Sent forward a detachment of 70 N.C.O.s & men to Ypres to take over portion of the semi wrecked Lunatic Asylum as billets for the unit & Hospital & dressing station for 84th Brigade. The building is in a state of ruin mostly; except the portion occupied by British Red + Society as Civil Hospital. They had 70 cases of civilians & many cases of injury as the results of the bombardment on Dec 21st last.	
2nd	Transport moved off at 7 pm by march route with Brigade Transport column & bivouacked at Outerdom	
2nd	Remainder of unit proceeded at daybreak by motor buses to Ypres. On arrival set to work to clear away debris & prepare FP for 200 cases & for their own billets. Captain Potter continued his duties as Sanitary Officer — men forbidden to drink the water before its being boiled.	

W 3299 200,000 (E) 8/14 J.B.C. & A. Forms/C. 2118/11.

Instructions regarding War Diaries and Intelligence Summaries are contained in F. S. Regs., Part II. and the Staff Manual respectively. Title pages will be prepared in manuscript.

WAR DIARY
or
INTELLIGENCE SUMMARY
(Erase heading not required.)

Army Form C. 2118.

Hour, Date, Place	Summary of Events and Information	Remarks and references to Appendices
February 3rd	Hospitals ready to receive cases. I went out to visit Regimental Aid Posts of the 4th Brigade at 6 p.m. Bearers under Capt Viall (Capt Fairbank & Lieut Rothkin went out at 8 p.m. to evacuate same with Motor Ambulance, brought in 8 cases. I made a second journey at 3.30 a.m. & brought in 25 wounded & 2 Officers 1/7 Northumberland Fusiliers wounded. 2nd/Lieut. L.R. MORTINHEAD & 2nd/Lieut. H.M. HEYDER both Shrapnel & slight. Major F.A. WHITE. 1st Suffolk admitted with Influenza & 24 other ranks.	
4th	Evacuated wounded 33 & sick 3. Officers Wounded 3. Admitted, ~~Officers~~ N.C.O.s & men wounded, ~~...~~ 44. I found necessary to carry the wounded ... from one of the Regimental Aid Posts ... of Rifle Bullet fire.	2/ Cheshire 6; 1/7 Northumberland Fus [illegible]; 1/ Welsh 2; 1/ Suffolk 1; 1/ R.F.A. 1; 4/ R. Fus 4; 7/E. Yorks 4; 1/ R.E. 1; 1/ Yorkshire 1

1247 W 3299 200,000 (E) 8/14 J.B.C. & A. Forms/C. 2118/11.

3

Instructions regarding War Diaries and Intelligence Summaries are contained in F. S. Regs., Part II. and the Staff Manual respectively. Title pages will be prepared in manuscript.

WAR DIARY
or
INTELLIGENCE SUMMARY

(Erase heading not required.)

Army Form C. 2118.

Hour, Date, Place	Summary of Events and Information	Remarks and references to Appendices
Feb 5th	Provided accommodation for about 300 patients [illegible] in case of emergency. Fatigue parties occupied in mending windows, building horse shelters for ambulances & improving sanitary condition of building & surroundings	
	Admitted, 1 Officer 2nd Lt. Miller 2/East Yorks wounded; 24 NCOs & men wounded & 12 sick	
	Evacuated 1 Officer & 38 NCOs & men. Died of wounds 1 NCO, 1 man	
6th	Several cases of self inflicted wounds having occurred asked ruling of A.D.M.S. as to disposal of them. He instructed that all such should be sent to the Field Ambulance at Ouderdom for Court of Enquiry as to whether wound was intentional or accidental & if latter whether unavoidable or due to [illegible] carelessness.	
	Admitted 21 NCOs & men sick & 24 wounded. Transferred 54 & discharged 6	
7th	Abdominal cases i.e. penetrating bullet wounds of abdomen doing well by keeping them here, some in Fowler position & others lying & avoiding any food or drink by mouth for 4 days but giving Rectal saline & nutrient injections morphia. 4 cases in now all doing well –	
	Admitted, wounded 24. Sick 135 of which 115 are Erythema Pernio, result of wet & cold in the trenches. Very few cases amongst officers & men who have kept feet dry by rubber boots or waders. Transferred to Clearing Station 52. Discharged to duty 44	

Instructions regarding War Diaries and Intelligence Summaries are contained in F. S. Regs., Part II. and the Staff Manual respectively. Title pages will be prepared in manuscript.

WAR DIARY
or
INTELLIGENCE SUMMARY
(Erase heading not required.)

Army Form C. 2118.

Hour, Date, Place	Summary of Events and Information	Remarks and references to Appendices
Feb 8th	Informed that Private Grigg of this unit in hospital at Hazebrouck is suffering from tetanus [illegible] by the [illegible]. He has had 2 inoculations (1500 cc) both in August last.	
	Admitted 22 wounded including 2 officers Capt. W.F. ANDERSON 3/Royal Fusiliers gunshot wound of abdomen & Major CROKER 1/Welsh Regt. Bronchitis, & 84 sick including 53 cases of Trench foot.	Transferred to A.P. 144; Discharged to duty 1; Died of wounds 1
9th	Put men to work making ~~[illegible]~~ palliasses for sick. Straw obtained locally. Found some difficulty in obtaining Brown Lamps locally for cleaning & lighting the hospital.	
	Capt. ANDERSON died of his wound, never rallied.	
	Admitted wounded 22. Sick 104, including 57 foot cases	
	Transferred to A.P. 90.	
10th	Admitted wounded 14 NCOs & men & 2/Lieut. E.S. NORTH 3/Royal Fus.; 2/Lieut. C. CAMPBELL 3/Middlesex Regt. & Sick 136 including 89 foot-cases	
	Transferred to A.P. 83. Discharged to Duty 61	
	Died. Capt. W.F. ANDERSON & one man	
11th	Admitted. Wounded 19 including Lieut. CORBETT-SINGLETON 2/Northumberland Fusiliers. Sick 306 including 279 foot cases & Major HINGLEY S.H. 3/Middlesex; Lieut. GORDON A.V. 3/ "; 2/Lieut. PECKHAM H. 7/E. Surrey; 2/Lieut. CUSTLER R.J.M. 3/Middlesex; Capt. MASON R.J. 3/Royal Fusiliers; Lieut. HODDING E.C. 3/Middlesex	
	Transferred to A.P. 313.	
	Discharged to Duty 34.	

5

Instructions regarding War Diaries and Intelligence Summaries are contained in F. S. Regs., Part II. and the Staff Manual respectively. Title pages will be prepared in manuscript.

WAR DIARY
or
INTELLIGENCE SUMMARY
(Erase heading not required.)

Army Form C. 2118.

Hour, Date, Place	Summary of Events and Information	Remarks and references to Appendices
February 12th	Admitted. wounded 9. Sick 44 including 38. feet cases. Transferred to AP. 61. discharged to duty 3. died 1.	
13th	Admitted wounded 22. Sick 102 including 72 feet cases + Capt. WILLCOX 1/Welsh - piles. Transferred to AP. 59. discharged to duty 3.	
14th	Admitted wounded 50. Sick 108 including 60. feet cases Transferred to AP. 134 - discharged to duty 3.	
15th	Admitted. wounded 92. including Capt. ROBINSON. A.C. 7/E. Surrey Lieut. SWINTON. G.E. " Lieut. CORKER W. " " EARL. N.V. 7/Buffs ~~2/Lieut~~ " MOLLER N.H. 3/Middlesex Capt. STUDD. L.F. 12/Co. of London Sick 90 including 51 feet cases + Lt-Col. MARTYN. A.R.S. 2/K.O.R.L. [illegible] Transferred to AP. 154. discharged to duty 66. died 3. including Capt. STUDD. L.F.	Lieut. BELL. IRVING 7/E Surrey " BEATTY. ~~[illegible]~~ G.D.H. " " HEALEY. A.G. " Capt. ANSON. E.S.G. " Maj. PORTER. C.L. 7/Buffs Capt. JUDKINS. L.E.H. 1/York & Lanc. Lieut. WARREN-DAVIS H.W. 1/Welsh
16th	Admitted. wounded 67. including ~~Lieut STEON, and 12/Co. of London~~ 2/Lieut. PAYNE. L.G.S. 1/Suffolks Capt. COOPER F.S. " Capt. CAMPBELL Lt-Col. ENDERBY S.H. 7/North'd Fus. Lieut. HERBERT. H.R. 3/Middlesex Sick 56. including 38 feet cases + Lieut. STEON. L.J. 17/Co. of London Lieut. BAXTER. E.H. 7/North'd Fus. Lieut. BARKWORTH. H.R. " " Lieut. WILKINS. D.A. 7/Buffs. Transferred to AP. 125. died 5. Discharged to duty 63.	

1247 W 3299 200,000 (E) 8/14 J.B.C. & A. Forms/C. 2118/11.

6

Instructions regarding War Diaries and Intelligence Summaries are contained in F. S. Regs., Part II. and the Staff Manual respectively. Title pages will be prepared in manuscript.

WAR DIARY
or
INTELLIGENCE SUMMARY
(Erase heading not required.)

Army Form C. 2118.

Hour, Date, Place	Summary of Events and Information	Remarks and references to Appendices
Feb 17th	Admitted. wounded 94. including Major BORRETT O.C. K.O.R.L. Lieut SAUNDERS H.C.R. 7/E. Yorks 2/" GUNN. S.W. " Capt. TRIMBLE. J.B.O "	
	Sick 85. including 57 foot cases + Major DOBSON. R.M. K.O.R.L. 2/Lieut FOY. F.J. "	
	Transferred to F.P. 92. died 2.	
	Discharged to duty 20.	
18th	Admitted. wounded 26 including Lieut LETHBRIDGE N.B. York + Lanc " LITCHFIELD. M.F. "	
	Sick 114. including 73 foot cases + Lieut HAMILTON. C.S.P. R.A.M.C. M.O. 7/Buffs Capt WALKER. P.S. 1/Suffolks Capt WILSON C.S. " Major WILSON. K.O.R.L.	
	Transferred to F.P. 68. died 2	
	Discharged to duty 99.	
19th	Admitted. wounded 16. including Capt. VISCOUNT EBRINGTON. Scots Guards Lieut KENNARD. P.N. 2/East Yorks	
	Sick 91. including 72 foot cases	
	Transferred to F.P. 70. died 2	
	Discharged to duty 63.	
	The wounded included a German prisoner belonging to the 105th Saxon Regiment, a schoolmaster by profession, who spoke English well [?] excellent condition physically & well clothed. G.S.W. of left arm & leg. He said their trenches were dry, floored, & pumped out daily.	

1247 W 3299 200,000 (E) 8/14 J.B.C. & A. Forms/C2118/11.

7.

Instructions regarding War Diaries and Intelligence Summaries are contained in F. S. Regs., Part II. and the Staff Manual respectively. Title pages will be prepared in manuscript.

WAR DIARY
or
INTELLIGENCE SUMMARY
(Erase heading not required.)

Army Form C. 2118.

Hour, Date, Place	Summary of Events and Information	Remarks and references to Appendices
February 20th	Admitted – wounded 9. Sick 32, including 16 foot-cases & { Lieut BARKWORTH H.J.P. / Capt LAMB. RM.	7/Northumberland F. / "
	Transferred to A.T. 53. Discharged to duty 28. Died 2	
21st	Admitted – wounded 67. including 2/Lieut HARRIS. G.G. 1/Roy West Kent. Sick 186. including 138 foot-cases & { Capt LAMBERT. K. KOYLI / Lt LYNCH-WHITE. 1/Roy W. Kent	
	Transferred to A.T. 122. Discharged to duty 36. Died 1.	
22nd	Admitted. wounded 19 including Capt MOLONY C.V. 1/Roy W. Kent. Sick 58 including 40 foot-cases & Lieut WILL. M.G. 7/Cheshire	
	Transferred to A.T. 76. Discharged to duty 39. Died 2.	
23rd	Bearers of the 86th (1/Northumbrian) Field Ambulance & 3 officers with 5 motor ambulances evacuated the Regimental aid post to relieve our men ~~[illegible]~~ ~~[illegible]~~	Cancelled
	Admitted. wounded 28. including 2/Lieut BURBERRY. J.J. 1/Roy W. Kent. Sick 11 including 6 foot-cases & Lieut PAYTON, [illegible]	/ "
	Transferred to A.T. 50. Discharged to duty 19 including { Capt LYNCH-WHITE / 2/Lieut HARRIS. G.G / Lieut WILL M.G.	
	Died 1 = 2/Lieut BURBERRY J.J.	

1247 W 3299 200,000 (E) 8/14 J.B.C. & A. Forms/C. 2118 11.

8/

Instructions regarding War Diaries and Intelligence Summaries are contained in F. S. Regs., Part II. and the Staff Manual respectively. Title pages will be prepared in manuscript.

WAR DIARY
or
INTELLIGENCE SUMMARY.
(Erase heading not required.)

Army Form C. 2118.

Hour, Date, Place	Summary of Events and Information	Remarks and references to Appendices
Feby 24th	Admitted wounded 34 { including 2/Lieut SLINGSBY H.L. 7/KOYLI; 2/ " HESS A.G. R.H.A; 2/ " HARRIS G.A. 1/Roy W. Kent; Lieut GRIFFIN H.J.G. Duke of Wellingtons	attached 31st Bde R.F.A
	Sick 24 including 2 foot cases	
	Transferred to A.T. 39	
	" to Conval. depot 5. Discharged to duty 5	
	Died 4 including 2/Lieut HESS A.G.	
25th	Visited by Col Sir Anthony Bowlby who approved of all our arrangements here — Regimental aid posts evacuated by the 88th Field Ambulance bearers & ambulances [illegible]	
	Admitted, wounded 9, including 2/Lieut HOOD A.F. 7/KOSB	
	Sick 44 including 11 foot cases & Lieut SLEIGH G.P. Duke of Wellingtons	
	Transferred to A.T. 33.	
	" to Conval. depot 5. Discharged to duty 17	
26th	Admitted wounded 11	
	Sick 28 including 13 foot cases & Capt BARNETT H.A. R.C. Chaplain attached 88th Field Ambce; 2/Lieut WOOLVEN W.S. 7/KOYLI	
	Transferred to A.T. 20	
	" to Conval. depot 17. Discharged to duty 14.	

9

Instructions regarding War Diaries and Intelligence Summaries are contained in F. S. Regs., Part II. and the Staff Manual respectively. Title pages will be prepared in manuscript.

WAR DIARY
or
INTELLIGENCE SUMMARY.
(Erase heading not required.)

Army Form C. 2118.

Hour, Date, Place	Summary of Events and Information	Remarks and references to Appendices
Feb 27th	Capt: BARNETT. H.A. R.C. chaplain attached. transferred to Casualty Clearing Station suffering from Influenza.	
	Capt: FOX H.W. C of E chaplain &	
	Capt: EVANS. J R.C. chaplain joined.	
	admitted wounded 21.	
	sick 15. including 4 feet cases	
	Transferred to A. 24	
	" Conval.t depot 19 . discharged to duty 5.	
28th	admitted wounded 13.	
	sick 11 including 7 feet cases & Lieut. SHELLEY. J.P. 2/K.O.R.L.	
	Transferred to A. 28	
	to Conval.t depot 6 discharged to duty 8. died 1.	
	Visited by a General on H.Q. Staff of 2nd Army. who looked over the whole building with a view to its being occupied by troops.	
	The 9th & 13th Brigades joined the Division on the 19th inst. It has been noticed that a very marked diminution of foot cases has occurred since – most probably chiefly due to the better physical condition of the men composing these Brigades	[signature] Lt Col O.C. 3rd London (85th) Field Ambulance 28th Division 28.2.15

121/5113
March 1915

121/5113

85th Field Ambulance

Vol III.

Bnd

Instructions regarding War Diaries and Intelligence Summaries are contained in F. S. Regs., Part II. and the Staff Manual respectively. Title pages will be prepared in manuscript.

WAR DIARY
or
INTELLIGENCE SUMMARY.
(Erase heading not required.)

Army Form C. 2118.

Hour, Date, Place	Summary of Events and Information	Remarks and references to Appendices
March 1st	11 of our horses are sick with ulceration round the coronet apparently due to infection from the soil. & 4 others are sick from irritant poisoning. 1 has died & post-mortem examination reveals inflammation of the intestinal mucosa.	
	Admitted wounded 24 including 2/Lieut. DISBRAME. H. 1/Lincolns, Lieut SHARP. F.A.H. 57 Dragoon Guards	
	Sick 37 including 9. foot cases	
	Transferred to P. 11	
	" to Conval. Depot. 0 discharged to Duty 7. Died 1	
2nd	– Major CLEMENTS. RAMC left to join his own unit the 17th Field Ambulance at AMENTIERE	
	Admitted. wounded 13	
	Sick 9 including 2 foot cases	
	Transferred to P 24	
	" to Conval depot. 8. discharged to Duty 2. Died 1	
3rd	– A Section took over Hospital Duties until 17th inst	
	Admitted. wounded 12	
	Sick 9. no foot cases	
	Transferred to P. 19.	
	" to Conval depot. 4 discharged to Duty 7.	

(73989) W4141—463. 400,000. 9/14. H.&J.Ltd. Forms/C. 2118/10.

2/

Instructions regarding War Diaries and Intelligence Summaries are contained in F. S. Regs., Part II. and the Staff Manual respectively. Title pages will be prepared in manuscript.

WAR DIARY
or
INTELLIGENCE SUMMARY.

(Erase heading not required.)

Army Form C. 2118.

Hour, Date, Place	Summary of Events and Information	Remarks and references to Appendices
March 4th	6 men joined unit from reinforcements	
	admitted wounded 11. including 7th	
	Sick 23 including 5 foot cases	
	Transferred to Clearing H. 12	
	" Conval: Depot 14th discharged to duty 1. Died 1.	
5th –	admitted wounded 17 including 2/Lt: CURSHAM, G. K.O.R.Lancs attached 1/R.W.Kents	
	Sick 27 including 1 foot-case	
	Transferred to Clearing H. 18. discharged to duty 5.	
	" Conval: Depot 13	
6th –	" admitted wounded 27 including Capt: WATSON, H.T. Kings Liverpool attached 7/KOYLI	
	Sick 8 including 1 foot-case + Lt Col HERRICK, H. RAMC 7/Cav Field Amb:	
	Transferred to Clearing H. 16	
	to Conval: Depot 10. discharged to Duty 6. Died 2 including Capt: WATSON, H.T.	
7th –	admitted wounded 15. including 2/Lt: BROADWAY, E.E. 7/K.O.S.B.	
	Sick 21. no foot cases + including Lt: FOSTER, F.G. RAMC attached 1/Cheshires	
	Transferred to Clearing H. 23	
	to Conval depot 4. discharged to duty 5	

3/

Instructions regarding War Diaries and Intelligence Summaries are contained in F. S. Regs., Part II. and the Staff Manual respectively. Title pages will be prepared in manuscript.

WAR DIARY
or
INTELLIGENCE SUMMARY.

(Erase heading not required.)

Army Form C. 2118.

Hour, Date, Place	Summary of Events and Information	Remarks and references to Appendices
March 8th	Admitted wounded 17	
	sick 62 including 39 foot-cases from 1/Cheshires who came out of trenches today.	
	Transferred to Clearing H. 28.	
	to Conval' Depot 42. Discharged to duty 2. Died 1.	
	Pt. DUTTON. W.A. 23 left the unit sick.	
9th	11 men joined from reinforcements.	
	3 men rejoined	
	Admitted wounded 14: including Maj: WICKHAM. T.E. R7a	
	Sick 27 including 6 foot-cases.	
	Transferred to Clearing H. 15.	
	to Conval' Depot 28 Discharged to duty 8.	
10th	Admitted wounded ~~12~~ (12)	
	sick 32 including 10 foot-cases & Capt: MOULTON-BARRETT 1/R. W. Kent.	E7.
	Transferred to Clearing H. 20.	
	Conval' Depot 11. Discharged to duty 7	
11th	Admitted wounded 4	
	sick 23 including 1 foot-case	
	Transferred to Clearing H. 14	
	to Conval' Depot nil Discharged to duty 4	
	arranged to detain a larger number of sick cases likely to be able to return to duty in a week or 10 days. in order to relieve the Convalescent Depot & prevent wastage.	

(73989) W4141—463. 400,000. 9/14. H.&J.Ltd. Forms/C. 2118/10.

4

Instructions regarding War Diaries and Intelligence Summaries are contained in F. S. Regs., Part II. and the Staff Manual respectively. Title pages will be prepared in manuscript.

WAR DIARY
or
INTELLIGENCE SUMMARY.
(Erase heading not required.)

Army Form C. 2118.

Hour, Date, Place	Summary of Events and Information	Remarks and references to Appendices
March 12th	admitted wounded 37. sick 33 including 1 foot case Transferred to Clearing H. 10 to Conval. Depot 1 Discharged to duty 13. Died 1	
13th	admitted wounded 30, including 2/Lt NEWBURY, H.G. 1/Lincolns sick 23 " Lt BATHER, E.J. RFA + 7 foot cases. Transferred to Clearing H. 27 " Conval. Depot 1. Discharged to duty 12. Died 1.	
14th	admitted wounded 30 including 2/Lt WHITE, L.S. 1/R.W. Kents sick 16 " 1 foot case Transferred to Clearing H. 26 Conval. Depot 2. Discharged to duty 27.	
15th	admitted wounded 17 sick 25 including Lt WHITE, H.P.W. RAMC attached RFA. Transferred to Clearing H. 33 " Conval. Depot 2. Discharged to duty 11. Died 3 including 2/Lt WHITE L.S. 1/R.W. Kent Foot cases practically cease from this date. On Feb 12th I caused enquiries to be made of 2nd & 9th French Army Corps as to their experience with foot cases, in order to compare same with our own experience — their answers to my questions I attach as an appendix.	

5

Instructions regarding War Diaries and Intelligence Summaries are contained in F. S. Regs., Part II. and the Staff Manual respectively. Title pages will be prepared in manuscript.

WAR DIARY
or
INTELLIGENCE SUMMARY.
(Erase heading not required.)

Army Form C. 2118.

Hour, Date, Place	Summary of Events and Information	Remarks and references to Appendices
March 16th	Lt SMITH. attached to 31st Brigade R.F.A. as M.O. to temporarily replace Lt WHITE. H.P.N. RAMC. sick.	
	Lt Col BIRRELL. RAMC called from G.H.Q. to ascertain my feeling on question of all R.A.M.C.T. reinforcements being pooled at the Base & deficiencies of any unit of R.A.M.C.T being supplied from this pool without reference to what unit they originally belonged. I disapproved on the ground that men join our own Reserve unit in order to come as reinforcements to this particular unit when needed.	
	Admitted wounded 16	
	sick 25 including 2/Lt WIGAN. W.L. 1/R.W. Kent, Lt HOLLAND. F. 10/Liverpool Scottish	
	Transferred to clearing H. 18	
	Conval depot 4 Discharged to Duty 10. Died 2	
17th	Lt SMITH. rejoined from duty with 31st Brigade R.F.A.	
	Sgt GREENSLADE & 5 men joined from reinforcement.	
	B. Section took over Hospital Duties.	
	Admitted wounded 16.	
	Sick 23. including 2 foot cases	
	Transferred to Clearing H. 16	
	Conval depot 1 Discharged to Duty. 4	
	Pte WHEELER. A.C. 37. left the unit sick	

(73989) W4141—463. 400,000. 9/14. H.&J.Ltd. Forms/C. 2118/10.

6

Instructions regarding War Diaries and Intelligence Summaries are contained in F. S. Regs., Part II. and the Staff Manual respectively. Title pages will be prepared in manuscript.

WAR DIARY
or
INTELLIGENCE SUMMARY.
(Erase heading not required.)

Army Form C. 2118.

Hour, Date, Place	Summary of Events and Information	Remarks and references to Appendices
March 18th	Drew 2 Riding Horses from remounts.	
	Admitted wounded 11	
	Sick 44 including Capt. ELLIS. T.M. 2/Duke of Wellingtons, Lt. KING. F.H. W. India Regt. attached 2/Duke of Wellingtons + 1 foot case	
	Transferred to Clearing H. 16	
	" Conval: Depot 1 Discharged to duty 25. Died 1.	
19th	Admitted wounded 5 including Lt. BURNYEAT. W.M. 1/Northumbrian Fusiliers	
	Sick 17 " 2/Lt. LLOYD W.E. 10/Liverpool Scottish	
	Transferred to Clearing H. 10 Discharged to duty 14.	
20th	Admitted wounded 8	
	Sick 14 including 2/Lt. SHEARMAN. H.H. 1/Lincolns, 2/Lt. BROOK L.T. 1/ " + 2 foot cases.	
	Transferred to Clearing H 13 Discharged to duty 13.	
21st	Admitted wounded 11	
	Sick 20 including Capt. PARTRIDGE. R.E. 1/Dorset	
	Transferred to Clearing H. 7 Discharged to duty 25.	
22nd	Admitted wounded 15 including Capt. MANSFIELD. H.S. R.F.A. + R.F.C	
	Sick 19 " 2/Lt. CLAYTON. J. G. 1/Dorset	
	Transferred to Clearing H. 15 + 2 foot cases	
	Conval: Depot 1 Discharged to duty 28 Died 1.	

Pte. JESSETT. J. 262 Transferred to Divisional Train for duty.
2 men joined from reinforcements from unit

(73989) W4141—463. 400,000. 9/14. H.&J.Ltd. Forms/C. 2118/10.

7

Instructions regarding War Diaries and Intelligence Summaries are contained in F. S. Regs., Part II. and the Staff Manual respectively. Title pages will be prepared in manuscript.

WAR DIARY
or
INTELLIGENCE SUMMARY.
(Erase heading not required.)

Army Form C. 2118.

Hour, Date, Place	Summary of Events and Information	Remarks and references to Appendices
March 23rd	Visited by Sir - - LAWLEY Governor of MADRAS on behalf of the Red + Society	
	Admitted Wounded 12	
	Sick 30	
	Transferred to Clearing H. 17	
	Convalt Dept. 0 Discharged to duty 17. Died 1.	
24th	Admitted Wounded 14.	
	Sick 28 including 1 foot case & Capt. BLAND. C.F. 2/K.O.S.B. Lt. LINDSAY. A.B. R.A.M.C attached 1/Dorsets.	
	Transferred to Clearing H. 13	
	Convalt Dept. 1 Discharged to duty 5.	
25th	Admitted Wounded 13	
	Sick 41 including 1 foot case & Capt. WESTLEY, G.H.A. 6/Liverpools Lt. PALMER. E.A. R.F.A.	
	Transferred to Clearing H. 10	
	Discharged to duty 26. Died 1.	
26th	Admitted Wounded 29 including Capt. MACDONA. E.V. R.F.A.	
	Sick 47 including 2 foot cases & Capt. NORMAN. R.G. A.S.C. 2/Lt. COOKES J.W. R.F.A.	
	Transferred to Clearing H. 26	
	Discharged to duty 25 Died 2.	

(73989) W4141—463. 400,000. 9/14. H.&J.Ltd. Forms/C. 2118/10.

9.

Instructions regarding War Diaries and Intelligence Summaries are contained in F. S. Regs., Part II. and the Staff Manual respectively. Title pages will be prepared in manuscript.

WAR DIARY
or
INTELLIGENCE SUMMARY.

(*Erase heading not required.*)

Army Form C. 2118.

1915 - Hour, Date, Place	Summary of Events and Information	Remarks and references to Appendices
March 31st	admitted wounded 17. Sick 70. including 2/Lt. WORMINGTON 1/Cheshire Lt. PAYNE. A. " Lt. BASSETT. F. L. 1/R. W. Kent	
	Transferred to Clearing Hosp 70 to Conval Depot 9 Discharged to duty 17 Died 1.	
	C. Section took over Hospital duties with 14th Div.	
	Total Admissions since opening at the Asylum Ypres on Feb 13th	
	Wounded 1279 Sick including 1374 Foot-cases 2672 3947	
	Classification of Wounds + Total Deaths in the Field Ambulance up to the end of March is as shown on accompanying chart.	appendix II
	[signature] Lt. Col O.C. 85th (3rd London) Field Ambulance 28th Division	

(73989) W4141—463. 400,000. 9/14. H.&J.Ltd. Forms/C. 2118/10.

Instructions regarding War Diaries and Intelligence Summaries are contained in F. S. Regs., Part II. and the Staff Manual respectively. Title pages will be prepared in manuscript.

WAR DIARY
or
INTELLIGENCE SUMMARY.
(Erase heading not required.)

Army Form C. 2118.

Hour, Date, Place	Summary of Events and Information	Remarks and references to Appendices
March 27th	Admitted wounded 25 Sick 30. including 4 foot cases Transferred to Clearing H. 36 discharged to duty 26	
28th	Admitted wounded 11 Sick 18 including 2/Lt HEDGES. W.H. - R.E. Transferred to Clearing H. 22. Discharged 18	
29th	Pte EDWARD. W.E. 215. of this unit. wounded in leg while on Bearer duty evacuating Regimental aid Post. Transferred to Clearing Hospital Admitted wounded 2. Sick 9. including 3 foot cases & Lt WILD. C.H. 1/R.W. Kents 2/Lt FARQUARSON. 1/Norfolks Transferred to Clearing H. 23 discharged to duty. 36	
30th	Admitted wounded 15 Sick 17 including 2/Lt POTTLE. W. 1/Bedfords Capt LILLY. C.O. 1/Dorsets Lt BATHER. E.J. R.F.A. Transferred to Clearing H. 7 discharged to duty 30.	

(73989) W4141—463. 400,000. 9/14. H.&J.Ltd. Forms/C. 2118/10.

Appendix II

N.B. The figures for fractures are in every case included in those of the parts injured.

Classification of Wounded

Admitted to 85th Field Ambulance between 4th Feb & 31st March (inclusive)

	Wounds of Head						Neck	Chest	Abdomen	Back			Arms						Legs							Total No Deaths	Total No Wounds
	Scalp	Skull	Brain	Face	Jaw	(fract^d)				Shoulder	Buttocks	Back	Humerous	fractured	Forearm	fractured	Hand	Fingers	Thigh	fractured	Knee	Lower leg	Fractured	Ankle	Foot		
Gunshot	83	68 9	11 5	68	7	(2)	35	31	27 12	67	22	36 6	51	(11)	88	(12)	79	63	89 4	(8)	21	54	(5)	9	40	36	949
Shrapnel	23	17 2		27	3	(1)	3	8 5	2 2	19	7	15	16		17	(2)	10	4	24 1	(3)	10	16 1	(2)	1	10	11	232
Grenade or Mortar	18	8		11			2 1	2		2	6	4	2		1	(1)	4 1		9 1		3	7	(1)	1	3	3	83
Accidental															1		4								1		6
Totals	124	93	11	106	10	(3)	40	41	29	88	35	55	69	(11)	107	15	97	67	122	(11)	34	77	(8)	11	54	50	1270

O.C. 85th F^d (3rd London) Field Amb^ce

appendix I

12/2/15.

Report on interview with D.M.S. of 9th French Army Corps, relative to Bad Feet

1	What proportion of bad feet did you have?	9th Army Corps (40,000), 3 to 4 cases a day of frozen feet with prospect of gangrene, & 30 to 40 cases a day of bad feet.
2	What were the different forms of bad feet?	No different forms, but different stages, & all due to "trophiques" troubles, & all presented oedeme & pain.
3	What were the causes? A. Frost! B. Moisture! C. Special microbe!	Both frost & moisture cause the trouble, & perhaps constriction of the ankle by the puttees. No special microbe has been discovered or suspected.
4	Means of prevention?	The use of fat of all description for the feet & boots, also large boots are advised. When possible in the trenches, the men should remove their boots once during the day, & massage their feet. Straw wrapped around the boots is also thought to be effective.
5	Cure?	Rest important. Massage, & large dressing of wool & bandaged. Also lie with feet raised.
6	Duration?	Average 2 to 3 weeks.
7	How long in trenches before symptom	Hard to say! Depends upon condition of men, & of trenches when taken over, also climatic conditions during stay.
8	Were trenches used by 9th Army Corps, old trenches, or dug by them?	These trenches were dug by 9th Army Corps. [N.B. Information from a Staff Officer, that a few were old British trenches dug during Oct. 1914.]

P.T.O.

(9) How long are the French troops in the trenches, & what period of rest?	4 days in, & 4 days rest

General remarks:

Whenever possible have wood flooring in trenches.
All of our men carry planks, or fagots, into trench with them.

Roger Ralse[?]
off. Interprète

Referred to in Diary of March 15th 1915

28th Division

121/6243

121/6243

April '15.

S

85th Field Ambulance

Vol IV

1

Instructions regarding War Diaries and Intelligence Summaries are contained in F. S. Regs., Part II. and the Staff Manual respectively. Title pages will be prepared in manuscript.

WAR DIARY
or
INTELLIGENCE SUMMARY.

(Erase heading not required.)

Army Form C. 2118.

Hour, Date, Place	Summary of Events and Information	Remarks and references to Appendices
1915 April 1st	Admitted wounded 16 including 2/Lieut CARTER. W. N. 9/London (Q.V.R)	
	Sick 29 including, fort-cont Lieut POTTINGER. R. D. RAMC attached 1/R. W. KENT	
	Transferred to Clearing H. 16 Discharged to duty 8	
2nd	Admitted wounded 11 including 2/Lieut CAWSTON. E. P. 9/London	
	Sick 34 including 2/Lieut ROBERTSON. E. 2/KOSB	
	Transferred to Clearing H. 24 Discharged to duty 24. Died 3	
3rd	Admitted wounded 16 including 2/Lieut LEWIS. A. N. 2/KOSB. 2/Lieut RENNY. G. M. RFA	
	Sick 15 Discharged to duty 25.	
	Transferred to Clearing H. 20.	
4th	Admitted wounded 16 including 2/Lieut PATERSON. W. P. 2/KOSB	
	Sick 28 including Capt HERAPATH. L. 2/Duke of Wellingtons Lieut FAIRBROTHER. C. B. 3/Lincolns attached 1st	
	Transferred to Clearing H. 27 Conval' depot 1 Discharged to duty 15. Died 1	

2/

Instructions regarding War Diaries and Intelligence Summaries are contained in F.S. Regs., Part II. and the Staff Manual respectively. Title pages will be prepared in manuscript.

WAR DIARY
or
INTELLIGENCE SUMMARY.
(Erase heading not required.)

Army Form C. 2118.

Hour, Date, Place	Summary of Events and Information	Remarks and references to Appendices
April 5th	Admitted wounded 23	
	Sick 32 including 2/Lieut. STREET. A. R.G.A.	
	Transferred to Clearing H. 11 Discharged to duty 12. Died 1	
	84th (2nd London) Field Ambulance joined us at the Asylum of the Sacred Heart to be accommodated for a few days	
6th	Admitted wounded 12	
	Sick 27	
	Transferred to Clearing H. 56 Discharged to duty 27	
	Ordered to evacuate as many cases as possible in view of moving into other quarters.	
7th	Admitted wounded 3	
	Sick 15	
	Transferred to Clearing H. 15 Discharged to duty 18.	
8th	Admitted Sick 1	
	Transferred to Clearing H. 17 Discharged to duty 29.	
	Advance Party under Capt. VICK moved to SOEURS. PENITENTS. CONVENT. RUE DE BRUGES POPERINGHE.	

(73989) W4141—463. 400,000. 9/14. H.&J.Ltd. Forms/C. 2118/10.

3

Instructions regarding War Diaries and Intelligence Summaries are contained in F. S. Regs., Part II. and the Staff Manual respectively. Title pages will be prepared in manuscript.

WAR DIARY
or
INTELLIGENCE SUMMARY.
(Erase heading not required.)

Army Form C. 2118.

Hour, Date, Place	Summary of Events and Information	Remarks and references to Appendices
1915 April 9th	Remainder of 'C' Section Tent Sub-Division moved to POPERINGHE to open up a Dressing Station at the Convent. Tent Subdivisions of A & B Sections & Headquarters moved into billets at same place. Bearers of A. B & C Sections moved into billets at YPRES.	
	Handed over Asylum to the 14th Field Ambulance.	
11th	Ordered to open a Dressing Station at School on ZONNEBEKE Road near VERLORENHOEK at point I.5.a.4.8. Detailed Capt. VICK with Lieut. ROBBINS & Lieut. SMITH R.V. & Tent Sub-division of 'C' Section for this duty.	
	Ordered to open up a Hospital for 350 beds at MALE ASYLUM near MENIN GATE, YPRES. Transferred Tent Subdivision of A Section to this Asylum to clean the place.	
	Admitted wounded 5 Sick 2 including 2/Lieut BRICKWOOD, A.C. 1/York Lancs.	

Instructions regarding War Diaries and Intelligence Summaries are contained in F. S. Regs., Part II. and the Staff Manual respectively. Title pages will be prepared in manuscript.

4

WAR DIARY
or
INTELLIGENCE SUMMARY.

(Erase heading not required.)

Army Form C. 2118.

Hour, Date, Place	Summary of Events and Information	Remarks and references to Appendices
1915		
April 12th	Moved remainder of unit from POPERINGHE to Lunatic Asylum YPRES. 'B' Section opened Hospital.	
	Admitted wounded 16 including Lieut. LETHBRIDGE N.D. 1/York & Lancs, Lieut. ROGERS W.H. 3/Middlesex	
	Sick 7	
	Transferred to Clearing H. 14 Died 2	
13th	Admitted wounded 12	
	Sick 9	
	Transferred to Clearing H. 13	
14th	Admitted wounded 49 including 2/Lieut. WEBSTER S. 1/York & Lancs	
	Sick 12	
	Transferred to Clearing H. 39 Discharged to Duty 4	
15th	Admitted wounded 4	
	Sick 19 Died 1	
	Transferred to Clearing H. 21	
16th	Admitted wounded 29 including 2/Lieut. HOUGHTON R.H. 1/KOYLI	
	Sick 33	
	Transferred to Clearing H. 13 Discharged to duty 9	
17th	Admitted wounded 12	
	Sick 5 including Lieut. BROADHURST S.H. R.F.A.	
	Transferred to Clearing H. 22 Discharged to duty 19, Died 1	

(73989) W4141—463. 400,000. 9/14. H.&J.Ltd. Forms/C. 2118/10.

5

Instructions regarding War Diaries and Intelligence Summaries are contained in F. S. Regs., Part II. and the Staff Manual respectively. Title pages will be prepared in manuscript.

WAR DIARY
or
INTELLIGENCE SUMMARY.
(Erase heading not required.)

Army Form C. 2118.

1915 Hour, Date, Place	Summary of Events and Information	Remarks and references to Appendices
April 18th	Admitted wounded 25 including 2/Lieut HOWARD. H.S. 1/4	1/York & Lancs
	Sick 20 including Major BEDWELL. E.P.	R.F.A.
	Lieut WAKEFIELD. T.D.	12/London Regt
	Transferred to Clearing H. 25	
	Discharged to Duty 12.	
19th	YPRES. severely bombarded with 17" shells, many falling close to hospital	
	Admitted wounded 36	
	Sick 15	
	Transferred to Clearing H. 52 Discharged to Duty 12	
20th	Admitted wounded 23	
	Sick 21	
	Transferred to Clearing H. 32 Discharged to Duty 14	
	Shelling still continues more or less continuously, most of the shells apparently passing over the hospital & aimed at the MENIN GATE & the GRAND PLACE	
21st	Detailed Bearers of 'C' Section to join their Tent Sub. Division at VERLORENHOEK in order to reinforce them & to have Bearers on the spot in an advanced position since it is obvious that the casualties are going to be numerous & that YPRES itself will have to be evacuated.	

Instructions regarding War Diaries and Intelligence Summaries are contained in F.S. Regs., Part II. and the Staff Manual respectively. Title pages will be prepared in manuscript.

6

WAR DIARY
or
INTELLIGENCE SUMMARY.
(Erase heading not required.)

Army Form C. 2118.

Hour, Date, Place	Summary of Events and Information	Remarks and references to Appendices
1915 April 21st contd	At 1 pm ordered to evacuate the Asylum (which we had just completed equipping for 350 beds) & to move back to POPERINGHE.	
	A & B Sections with Transport of C Section marched at 4.30 pm & billeted in tents in small field behind a School in RUE BASSIN, POPERINGHE, the Transport being billeted in ground of convent of SOEURS PENITENTS close by.	
	Admitted at VERLORENHOEK and YPRES	
	wounded 48 including 2/Lieut BEVIR, C.F.T., RHA, Lieut THOMAS, R.L.C. [illegible]	
	Sick 17 including Lieut LOMAX R. R.F.A.	
	Transferred to Clearing R. 99	
	discharged to duty 8. died 1	
22nd	The Germans used gas for first time against French on our left from GRAVENSTAFEL northwards especially against junction of British & French line with result that the line broke.	
	The first news of it was obtained from a number of French Algerian & Moroccan soldiers who apparently arrived the Grand Place at POPERINGHE about 7.45 pm together with some G.S. Wagons full of	

(73989) W4141—463. 400,000. 9/14. H.&J.Ltd. Forms/C. 2118/10.

Instructions regarding War Diaries and Intelligence Summaries are contained in F. S. Regs., Part II. and the Staff Manual respectively. Title pages will be prepared in manuscript.

WAR DIARY
or
INTELLIGENCE SUMMARY.
(Erase heading not required.)

Army Form C. 2118.

7.

Hour, Date, Place	Summary of Events and Information	Remarks and references to Appendices
1915 April 22nd	French soldiers who were lying upon each other groaning & moaning & all very exposed. The Bearers & Motor Ambulances were despatched to the Dressing Station as usual at 9.20 pm to go to the Regtl Aid Posts at VERLORENHOEK & thence to evacuate same. but returned within half an hour with information that the road was blocked E of POPERINGHE & they were unable to get through. At 11 pm I proceeded to Divisional Head Quarters at VLAMERTINGHE CHATEAU to obtain orders. ADMS instructed me to stand by & not to send forward Bearers or Ambulances until he sent me orders. At 1.30 am not having received orders I again proceeded to Divisional Headquarters & took all the available Bearers & Motor Ambulances with me. The road was still very much blocked with refugees, & their cattle & belongings. ~~[illegible]~~ fleeing towards POPERINGHE & troops French & Algerian with guns & transport.	

Instructions regarding War Diaries and Intelligence Summaries are contained in F. S. Regs., Part II. and the Staff Manual respectively. Title pages will be prepared in manuscript.

8.

WAR DIARY
or
INTELLIGENCE SUMMARY.
(Erase heading not required.)

Army Form C. 2118.

Hour, Date, Place	Summary of Events and Information	Remarks and references to Appendices
April 22nd	As there was no time to spare if the aid Post was to be evacuated before daybreak. I asked for & obtained loan of A.D.M.S. to try to get the Bearers & ambulances through to VERLORENHOEK and on to ZONNEBEKE via ST JEAN. As YPRES was in flames & being heavily shelled with much difficulty this was accomplished. At the Dressing Station I found a large number of wounded including French, Algerians, Canadians & Belgians. Lieut. R.F. BARNSLEY of this unit was wounded in thigh by rifle bullet while out with the Bearers at ZONNEBEKE.	
	Admitted wounded 99 including Lieut HINCH HAYCOCK. R.A. 1/KOYLI " WORTON. J. 3/Monmouths " BARNSLEY. R.F. 85th (3rd London) Field Ambulance	
	Sick 20 Transferred to Clearing H. 119	
	During the night we were all embarrassed at our work by the irritation of the eyes produced by gas which penetrated into the Dressing Station.	

9

Instructions regarding War Diaries and Intelligence Summaries are contained in F. S. Regs., Part II. and the Staff Manual respectively. Title pages will be prepared in manuscript.

WAR DIARY
or
INTELLIGENCE SUMMARY.
(Erase heading not required.)

Army Form C. 2118.

Hour, Date, Place	Summary of Events and Information	Remarks and references to Appendices
1915 April 23rd	By 5 am the wounded all having been dressed & fed it became evident that the Dressing Station would have to be evacuated, as shells were [illegible] falling near & I arranged for the wounded to be conveyed to the fields & near Brielen [?] [illegible] & then returned through YPRES to POPERINGHE to [illegible] and forward all our horse ambulances to evacuate the wounded. While the patients were being removed to the field the Dressing Station was shelled & 4 wounded were killed during the [illegible] cases. The remainder were taken charge by our own & Red Cross ambulances.	
	Admitted wounded 100 including Capt. Taylor, A. 9/Roy. Scots [?]	
	" BELL, D 9 " "	
	Lieut. CROUKSHANKS, A. C. RFA [?]	
	2/Lt. CHAMBERLAIN, J. [illegible]	
	2/Lt. CONNELL, W. [illegible]	
	Killed 7	
	Transferred to Clearing H. 108	
	The incident recorded in separate appendix which occurred to-day, is worthy of record to the credit of the 3 Bearers concerned	See appendix

(73989) W4141—463. 400,000. 9/14. H.&J.Ltd. Forms/C. 2118/10.

10

Instructions regarding War Diaries and Intelligence Summaries are contained in F. S. Regs., Part II. and the Staff Manual respectively. Title pages will be prepared in manuscript.

WAR DIARY
or
INTELLIGENCE SUMMARY.
(Erase heading not required.)

Army Form C. 2118.

Hour, Date, Place	Summary of Events and Information	Remarks and references to Appendices
1915 April 24th	Dressing Station evacuated & moved back to an Estaminet near POTYZE.	
	Our camp at POPERINGHE & the town bombarded from direction of BOESINGHE with 6in shells. Driver REWCASTLE killed & Driver WASHER wounded & several horses wounded & 1 ambulance wagon smashed	
	Admitted wounded 72	
	Sick 3	
	Transferred to Clearing H. 75	
25th	Admitted wounded 231 including Major BALLANTINE. J	4/Canadians
	Capt. PERCY. H.M.D.	Canadian F.A.
	Lieut. PICK. P.W.	1/Canadians
	" GRINDELL. G.W.	4/East Yorks
	2/Lieut. MALLALIEU. W.	R.F.A.
	2/ " ELLIS. J.W.L.	2/[illegible]
	2/ " HORSLEY. S.S.	2/[illegible]
	2/ " BROWN. J.C.	5/Durham L.I.
	Sick 32	
	Transferred to Clearing H. 262 Died 1	
	Lieut. R.V. Smith & party in charge of Dressing Station to-night. Relieved at 10 pm. by Major Walker who will be on duty till tomorrow night.	

(73989) W4141—463. 400,000. 9/14. H.&J.Ltd. Forms/C. 2118/10.

Instructions regarding War Diaries and Intelligence Summaries are contained in F. S. Regs., Part II. and the Staff Manual respectively. Title pages will be prepared in manuscript.

11

WAR DIARY
or
INTELLIGENCE SUMMARY.

(Erase heading not required.)

Army Form C. 2118.

Hour, Date, Place	Summary of Events and Information	Remarks and references to Appendices
1915		
April 26th	POPERINGHE bombarded by 13" shells.	
	Admitted wounded 431 including Major MOULTON-BARRETT, E.N.	2/North'd Fusiliers
	" CAMERON, J. S.T.	9/Roy Scots
	" MERCEREAU, C.J.	H.Q. 2/Canadian Inf Brigade
	Capt. MORRILL T.J.	4/E. Yorks
	" IDRIS W.	3/Roy Fus
	" NATION R.?	3/ " "
	" JACKS H.	7/Durham
	Lieut DUNLOP W.	2/E. Surrey
	" HARRIS G.N.	5/Canadians
	" ANDERSON C.E.L.	107/Sikhs
	" CARRICK H.M.	4/North'd Fus
	" WILLIAMS O.	1/Monmouth
	2/Lieut LE MARCHANT S.	3/Roy Fus
	2/ " DANKIN F.O.	7/North'd "
	2/ " DADDS H.?	5/ " "
	2/ " ANDERSON F.G.	1/Monmouth
	2/ " COLLINS E.W.	2/Shropshire
	2/ " HOPPER H.	7/Durham L.I.
	+ 4 German Prisoners.	
	Sick 0	
	Transferred to Clearing H. 424. Died 3.	
27th	POPERINGHE being still bombarded & already evacuated by civil population & clearing H.s ordered to move the unit to a FARM 1 mile E of POPERINGHE.	
	The Dressing Station at POTYZE to be run now by a small staff of 1 Officer & 8 or 12 men on duty for 24 hours as it is under constant shell fire. & supplemented by	

(73989) W4141—463. 400,000. 9/14. H.&J.Ltd. Forms/C. 2118/10.

12.

Instructions regarding War Diaries and Intelligence Summaries are contained in F.S. Regs., Part II. and the Staff Manual respectively. Title pages will be prepared in manuscript.

WAR DIARY
or
INTELLIGENCE SUMMARY.
(Erase heading not required.)

Army Form C. 2118.

Hour, Date, Place	Summary of Events and Information	Remarks and references to Appendices
1915		
April 27th	other officers & personnel at night while the Aid post are being evacuated	
	Captain VICK. S/Sgt BOYLES & 8 men on duty to night	
	Admitted wounded 400 including Major MATTHEWS. H.H.	6/D.L.I.
	" GRIFFITHS D.M.	R.E.
	Lieut OVIONS W.	3/Monmouths
	Capt. WALTON. F.	6/D.L.I.
	2/Lieut NICHOLSON. H.M.	6/ " "
	2/ " TURNER. D.T.	4/ North'd F.
	2/ " HUGHES. H.A.M.	1/Suffolks
	2/ " BUTCHER. T.A.	4/K.R.R.
	Transferred to Clearing Sick 12 / H. 410 Died 9.	
28th	The Dressing Station shelled out of the Estaminet & moved to some Cottages a little W of it.	
	Captain POTTER on duty to night.	
	Admitted wounded 516 including Lieut HARVEY. B.S.	1/Monmouths
	" CAPEL. E.	5/London
	" WOOD. D.T.	1/Suffolks
	2/ " JAMES. W.M.	1/Monmouths
	Transferred to Clearing Sick 50 / H. 563. Died 3.	

13/

Instructions regarding War Diaries and Intelligence Summaries are contained in F. S. Regs., Part II. and the Staff Manual respectively. Title pages will be prepared in manuscript.

WAR DIARY
or
INTELLIGENCE SUMMARY.
(Erase heading not required.)

Army Form C. 2118.

Hour, Date, Place	Summary of Events and Information	Remarks and references to Appendices
1915 April 29th	Admitted wounded 116 Capt PARK. R.D. 6/ R.D.F. " CUMMINS. A.P. 6/ " " VILLIERS-STUART P.G. 2/Cheshires " OTTER. R.E. 5/London 2/Lieut BEARD. H.C. 5/ " 2/ " ETHELSTONE. S. R.F.A. Sick 12 Transferred to Clearing Hosp. 125 Died 2. Dressing Station taken over by 86th Field Ambulance. Dressing Station taken over by 86th Field Ambulance but our Bearers did not evacuate Aid Post but 1 Officer 2 NCOs & 3 Bearers went out as guides to the 86th Field Amb. to shew them the Posts & found without Motor Ambulances it would have been practically impossible to have cleared the Aid Posts & evacuated the numbers of wounded with which we had to deal since the 22nd owing that it was impossible to do any of this work during daylight whereas at night the ambulances were able to get as far forward as ZONNEBEKE	

14

Instructions regarding War Diaries and Intelligence Summaries are contained in F. S. Regs., Part II. and the Staff Manual respectively. Title pages will be prepared in manuscript.

WAR DIARY
or
INTELLIGENCE SUMMARY.
(Erase heading not required.)

Army Form C. 2118.

Hour, Date, Place	Summary of Events and Information	Remarks and references to Appendices
1915 April 30th	Orders to move the unit to HOOGE GRAAF 2 miles S. of POPERINGHE tomorrow. Later to open up a Hospital for 200 in a School for seriously wounded & in a Camp for slighter cases –	
	1 Officer with 4 Motor Ambulances & Drivers & 4 Orderlies rendezvoused at Town Hall POPERINGHE at 8pm to join the convoy of ambulances to evacuate the Dressing Stations of the 28th Division.	
	Lieut. J. TAYLOR with 1 Motor Ambulance & 6 Bearers & 2 Drivers paraded at 7.30 pm & proceeded to ST JEAN to conduct the evacuation of wounded to POPERINGHE.	See Appendix II
	Classification of wounds treated & total deaths in the Field Ambulance for month of April is as shown in accompanying Chart. Appendix III	[illegible signature] Lt. Col. O.C. 85th (3rd London) Field Ambulance
	Total admissions for April: Sick 510, Wounded 1410, Gas Asphyxiated 26 = 1946. Total since Feb 3rd: Sick 3182, Wounded 2680, Gas Asphyx 26 = 5888	

APPENDIX II

N.B. THE FIGURES FOR FRACTURES ARE IN EVERY CASE INCLUDED IN THOSE OF THE PART INJURED.

CLASSIFICATION of WOUNDED.

ADMITTED TO 85TH FIELD AMBULANCE DURING THE MONTH OF APRIL 1915.

	WOUNDS of HEAD						NECK	CHEST	ABDOMEN	BACK			ARMS.						LEGS.							TOTAL Nº DEATHS	TOTAL Nº WOUNDS.
	SCALP	SKULL	BRAIN	FACE	JAW.	fract.				BACK	SHLDRS	BUTTKS	HUMERUS	fract.	FOREARM	fract.	HAND	FINGERS	THIGH	fract.	KNEE	LOWER LEG	fract.	ANKLE	FOOT		
GUNSHOT	26	60 7	2.	39	2	(1)	22.	27 4	17 6	20	33	23	42	(3)	62	(6.)	52	33	66.	(10)	13	48	(5)	8	35	17	630
SHELL.	48	26		37	4		14	21	9 3	40	43	35	49	(4)	30	(2)	30	14	92 4	(7)	33	74 3	(10)	16	36,	10	651
GRENADE OR MORTAR	7	3		13			2	1	4 1	4	7	3	2	(1)	6	(1)	4	2	14	(1)	3	18 1	(4)	2	7	2	102
ACCIDENT.																	5						–	1			6
TOTALS.	81	89 7	2	89	6	(1)	38	49 4	30 10	64	83	61	93	(8)	98	(9)	91	49	172 4	(18)	49	140 4	(19)	27.	78	29	1389.

APRIL. 1915.

II

APPENDIX I to page 9. April 1915

Record of incident on April 23rd

On this date one of our Motor Ambulances was proceeding over the MENIN BRIDGE with several Bearers returning to POPERINGHE when a shell burst in rear of it. The Bearers seeing that an Ammunition wagon team & drivers had been hit, stopped the Ambulance got out & found the team of 6 horses & several men lying in the road. The horses were shot by an Artillery Officer who was passing & the Bearers dressed the injured men under shell fire. & placed all but one of them in the Ambulance & sent them on to POPERINGHE

Pte STEPHENS. P.M. No 182. then made his way across the Bridge - which was being heavily shelled - into a house previously used by a Medical Unit, searched for & found some Morphia & a hypodermic syringe, then returned to the remaining wounded man who was dying in great agony from an abdominal wound from which his intestines extruded. & gave him a dose of morphia. The 3 Bearers then carried him into shelter of a neighbouring house & stood by for some time until he died.

The whole work was performed under heavy fire from high explosive shells, which were bursting within a few yards - as was their subsequent progress back through YPRES.

The names of the Bearers are

Pte STEPHENS. P.M. 182
Pte MATTHEWS. W.F. 23
Pte PIPER .76

[illegible]
Lt. Col.

28th Division

121/6243.

121/6243

May 15.

S

85th Field Ambulance

Vol V

Instructions regarding War Diaries and Intelligence Summaries are contained in F. S. Regs., Part II. and the Staff Manual respectively. Title pages will be prepared in manuscript.

WAR DIARY
or
INTELLIGENCE SUMMARY.
(*Erase heading not required.*)

Army Form C. 2118.

Hour, Date, Place	Summary of Events and Information	Remarks and references to Appendices
1915 May 1st	The unit moved to HOOGE GRAET + opened Hospital in the School + in Camp for sick. Personnel billeted in Barns + Officers under Canvas. Admitted sick 3. Transferred to clearing H. 2 discharged to duty 1.	[illegible]
2nd + 3rd	Occupied arranging Hospital Camp. Received from British Red + Society 3 (per section) large [illegible] + [illegible] No 3 size PRIMUS Stoves + which I asked them while at YPRES + which could not be obtained from Ordnance. The smaller ones in the equipment were quite inadequate to supply the quantity of Hot water required when dressing large numbers of cases.	[illegible]
3rd	Was informed of the G.O.C.s disposition for withdrawing the line of posts from ZONNEBEKE to the FREZENBERG ridge at 1.30 am. Then [illegible] for the evacuation of wounded from all the Aid Posts by 12-30 am. + our being clear VERLOREN HOEK [illegible] 100 Bearers + all our Ambulances [illegible] Horse to ZONNEBEKE all the posts were under Capt FAIRBANK, Lieut ROBBINS + Lieut TAYLOR.	[illegible] NCO. & 6 [illegible] St JEAN + FORTUIN [illegible] POPERINGHE

Instructions regarding War Diaries and Intelligence Summaries are contained in F. S. Regs., Part II. and the Staff Manual respectively. Title pages will be prepared in manuscript.

2

WAR DIARY

or

INTELLIGENCE SUMMARY.

(Erase heading not required.)

Army Form C. 2118.

Hour, Date, Place	Summary of Events and Information	Remarks and references to Appendices
May 3rd	completely cleared up to time, except the HAMPSHIRE'S which being very difficult to find & no guide sent to [illegible] Lieut. J. TAYLOR therefore was not reached in time to entirely evacuate by the hour fixed. Lieut TAYLOR however worked hard at the [illegible] half an hour after he should have done, but ultimately had to leave several very badly wounded, being [illegible] all of whom were not likely to live [illegible] with two Regimental Stretchers. [illegible] to [illegible] by the GERMANS. both after [illegible] – to be taken over by the GERMANS The ultimate readjustment of the line was accomplished without a casualty.	

[illegible] R.F.A.

3/

Instructions regarding War Diaries and Intelligence Summaries are contained in F. S. Regs., Part II. and the Staff Manual respectively. Title pages will be prepared in manuscript.

WAR DIARY
or
INTELLIGENCE SUMMARY.
(Erase heading not required.)

Army Form C. 2118.

Hour, Date, Place	Summary of Events and Information	Remarks and references to Appendices
1915 May 4th	Admitted wounded 3 including 2/Lieut BENHAM. J.A. R.F.A. (died)	
	Transferred to Clearing H 2 died 1	
	Capt: RM VICK with 44 Bearers, 4 Motor Ambulances & 5 [illegible]	
	[illegible] & proceeded to the White Chateau POTIJZE, there to	
	pick up [illegible] to the Regl. Aid Posts of 83rd & 84th Brigades	
	at 9 pm. The Aid Posts on the front from SHELLTRAP FARM	
	north of WIELTJE to BELLEWARDE FARM were cleared &	
	wounded evacuated to Dressing Station of 84th Field Amb[illegible]	
	in the cellars of the Asylum of the [illegible] YPRES	
	When the whole area had been cleared the Ambulances	
	proceeded to clear the Dressing Station back to	
	POPERINGHE.	
	Major WAGGETT reported at Town Hall POPERINGHE at	
	11.30 pm to [illegible] as Convoy regulating Officer.	
	The G.O.C. Lieut General BULFIN [illegible] an Order [illegible]	
	to express to all the personnel concerned his high appreciation	
	of the manner in which the 28th Division [illegible]	
	cleared of wounded on the night May 3-4	
5th	Admitted Wounded 33	
	Sick 20	
	Gas asphyxiated 1	
	Transferred to Clearing H 33.	

(73989) W4141—463. 400,000. 9/14. H.&J.Ltd. Forms/C. 2118/10.

Instructions regarding War Diaries and Intelligence Summaries are contained in F. S. Regs., Part II. and the Staff Manual respectively. Title pages will be prepared in manuscript.

WAR DIARY
or
INTELLIGENCE SUMMARY.
(Erase heading not required.)

Army Form C. 2118.

4/3

Hour, Date, Place	Summary of Events and Information	Remarks and references to Appendices
1915		
May 6th	Admitted Sick 5	
7th	Received orders to prepare to take in wounded. Arranged for 'B' Section, under Major WAGGETT, to run the School Hospital for Sick + 'C' Section under Captain VICK to run the Camp Hospital for wounded. 3 Operating Tents + 30 Bell Tents (12 borrowed from 84th + 6 from 86th Field Ambulance)	
	Admitted wounded 9 including Capt. ATKINSON. E. 5/K.O.R.L., 2/Lieut TAYLOR. R.V. 2/North'd Fus.	
	Sick 23 Gas Asphyxiated 1 — Discharged to Duty 4	
8th	Admitted wounded 251 including Major LEWIS, C.S.A. 3/Monmouth; Capt. BOLS. J. 2/KORL; " TATTERSALL 12/London; Lieut. DUNLOP. J.K. 12/ "; " DERRY. R.M. 3/Monmouth; 2/" LLOYD. T.J.L. 3/ "; 2/" SORBY. C.M.C. 3/; 2/" HORNE. A.W.M. 2/KORL; 2/ NEWINGTON. K. 3/E. Surrey attd 1/Welsh	
	Sick 55 Gas Asphyxiated 3	
	Transferred to Clearing H. 254 — Discharged to duty 11 — Died 1	

(73989) W4141—463. 400,000. 9/14. H.&J.Ltd. Forms/C. 2118/10.

Instructions regarding War Diaries and Intelligence Summaries are contained in F. S. Regs., Part II. and the Staff Manual respectively. Title pages will be prepared in manuscript.

5 #

WAR DIARY
or
INTELLIGENCE SUMMARY.
(Erase heading not required.)

Army Form C. 2118.

Hour, Date, Place	Summary of Events and Information	Remarks and references to Appendices
1915 May 9th	Joined & added to Strength today No 3250 Pte BIGGS G.W.	
	" 3254 " BRUFORD W.E.	
	" 3257 " JARRETT W.J.	
	" 3258 " STUBBS F.H.	
	" 3267 " WEST A.A.	
	Sent out all Motor & Horse Ambulances to [illegible] & [illegible] Reg Aid Posts.	
	Admitted wounded 408 including Major PIGGE W.N. 2/E. Yorks	
	Capt. NORTHCOTE. 1/E. Surrey	
	" EDWARDS B.M. 4/ R.Berks	
	" BAINBRIDGE J 5/ KORL	
	Lieut. SEWARD. A.S. 5/ "	
	" ROWE. A. 5/ "	
	" MORSHEAD. L.J. RE.	
	" MARRECK. J.R. RAMC attd 1/Monmouths	
	" McLEAN. G.D. RAMC " 3/ "	
	" HEBBURN. C.J. 1/Monmouths	
	" NEWMAN. A.C. 2/Cheshires	
	" HERBERT. H.R. 3/Middlesex	
	2/Lieut. FLETCHER. G.H.F. 8/ "	
	" CORBET G. 1/Suffolk	
	" SOMERVILLE. G.R. 2/KORL	
	" TODD. J.H. 5/ "	
	" KYLE. J.S. 2/E. Yorks	
	" OWBRIDGE W.W. 1/KOYLI	
	" TROWBRIDGE. T.S.W. 4/K.R.R	
	Sick 40 → including 2/Lieut STOYLE. E.G. RFA	
	" TOLLEMACHE. H.R. 2/Camerons	
	for Asphyxiated 3	
	Transferred to Clearing H. 392	
	Died 12.	

Instructions regarding War Diaries and Intelligence Summaries are contained in F. S. Regs., Part II. and the Staff Manual respectively. Title pages will be prepared in manuscript.

6

WAR DIARY
or
INTELLIGENCE SUMMARY.
(Erase heading not required.)

Army Form C. 2118.

Hour, Date, Place	Summary of Events and Information	Remarks and references to Appendices
May 10th	Lieut. WOOTTON. L.H. joined & was taken on the strength.	
	Admitted wounded 245 including Major ARCHER-SHEE. M. 19/Hussars	
	Capt. CARTON de WIART. A. 4/D.G.	
	" RAFFLES 3/R. Welsh Fus.	
	Lieut. GIBB. JHP 4/DG	
	" LAWRENCE. AE 4/KRR	
	" HEFFERMAN R.A.M.C. att'd 3/R. Welsh Fus.	
	2/Lieut. LONERGAN. H. 2/E. Surrey	
	" WASHINGTON. R. N. Staffords att'd 2/Cambridgeshire	
	" NEWELL. T.S. 2/Cheshire	
	" CLANTON 2/ [illegible]	
	" KING. RA.F.S. 2/	
	" WYNDHAM. G.R.C. 3/K.R.R	
	Sick 31 including 2/Lieut ECKSTEIN. B 3/E. Surrey att'd 2/E. Surrey	
	Gas asphyxiated 3	
	Transferred to Clearing H. 361 discharged to duty 4. Died 2	
11th	Admitted wounded 89 including Capt. GOLDNEY. H.W. 31 Heavy Bty R.G.A.	
	Lieut. GARNER. W. 8/Middlesex	
	Sick 36 including Lt/Col WORSLEY-GOUGH. H.W. 3/Monmouth	
	2/Lieut. HILLS. A 2/Cambridgeshire	
	Gas asphyxiated 1	
	Transferred to Clearing H. 134 discharged to duty 16 died 3.	

(73989) W4141—463. 400,000. 9/14. H.&J.Ltd. Forms/C. 2118/10.

7

Instructions regarding War Diaries and Intelligence Summaries are contained in F. S. Regs., Part II. and the Staff Manual respectively. Title pages will be prepared in manuscript.

WAR DIARY
or
INTELLIGENCE SUMMARY.
(*Erase heading not required.*)

Army Form C. 2118.

Hour, Date, Place	Summary of Events and Information	Remarks and references to Appendices
1915		
May 12th	Admitted wounded 60 including Lieut CHAPMAN. W.W. 2/Buffs, " MORGAN. H. de R. 2/ ", 2/Lieut. FALCONER-STEWART. C. 9/Roy Scots	
	Sick 20	
	Gas asphyxiation 1	
	Transferred to Clearing H. 79 discharged to duty 10. Died 3	
13th	Admitted wounded 34 including Capt. WILSON. H.S. anti-aircraft gun section (att.)	
	Sick 58	
	Transferred to Clearing H. 55 discharged to duty 3. Died 3	
	Captain Bt. POTTER detailed to visit the units resting in 84th Brigade area daily to collect their sick & bring them into Hospital.	
14th	Admitted wounded 0	
	Sick 8 including Capt. HOUBLON. H. A. 2/Buffs	
	Transferred to Clearing H. 41 discharged to duty 4	
15th	Admitted wounded 2	
	Sick 20	
	Transferred to Clearing H. 8 discharged to duty 1 died 1	
	No. 032076 Pte. HARRISON. C. M.T. A.S.C. joined & taken on strength as Motor cyclist.	

(73989) W4141—463. 400,000. 9/14. H.&J.Ltd. Forms/C. 2118/10.

Instructions regarding War Diaries and Intelligence Summaries are contained in F. S. Regs., Part II. and the Staff Manual respectively. Title pages will be prepared in manuscript.

8

WAR DIARY
or
INTELLIGENCE SUMMARY.
(Erase heading not required.)

Army Form C. 2118.

Hour, Date, Place	Summary of Events and Information	Remarks and references to Appendices
May 16th	Admitted Sick 21	
	Transferred to Clearing H 12 Discharged to duty 1	
17th	Admitted wounded 1	
	Sick 6	
	Transferred to Clearing H 11 Discharged to duty 2	
18th	Admitted Sick 8	
	Transferred to Clearing H 6 Discharged to duty 3	
19th	Admitted Sick 40 Discharged to duty 4	
	Following men joined & were taken on strength from ROUEN	
	No 1777 Pte HARRIS. F.L.	
	1766 " COOK. I.A.	
	1609 " LINNETT. C.	
	1765 " FRENCH. J.	
	1725 " BROWNE. F.W.	
	1787 " HORROCKS. G.A.	
	1792 " VINER. A.	
	1747 " SAWYERS. A.A.	
20th	Admitted Sick 11 Discharged to duty 6	
21st	Admitted Sick 89 including Capt. KITCHIN. C 3/Middlesex, 2/Lieut. WOLFENDALE W.A. 5/K.O.R.L.	
	gas asphyxiated 1	
	Transferred to Clearing H 10 Discharged to Duty 5	

(73989) W4141—463. 400,000. 9/14. H.&J.Ltd. Forms/C. 2118/10.

Instructions regarding War Diaries and Intelligence Summaries are contained in F. S. Regs., Part II. and the Staff Manual respectively. Title pages will be prepared in manuscript.

9

WAR DIARY
or
INTELLIGENCE SUMMARY.
(Erase heading not required.)

Army Form C. 2118.

Hour, Date, Place	Summary of Events and Information	Remarks and references to Appendices
1915 May 22nd	Motor Ambulances with bearing parties under 2 officers + 2 NCOs reported at Asylum YPRES at 9pm to proceed to evacuate Reg. aid Posts at POTYZE CHATEAU + ECOLE OR [illegible] [illegible] on MENIN ROAD	
	Admitted Sick 50 including Capt. McEWAN OR RAMC	attd 2/Cheshires
	Transferred to Clearing H. 40 Discharged to duty 49	
23rd	2 Motor Ambulances with 12 Bearers under Lieut ROBBINS evacuated Reg. aid Posts	
	Admitted wounded 47	
	Sick 43	
	gas asphyxiated 2	
	Transferred to Clearing H. 76 Discharged to duty 17.	
24th	5 motor ambulances + 100 men under 1 officer 55 Bearers. 5 motor ambulances rendezvoused at Asylum YPRES + proceeded to evacuate aid Posts at 8.20 pm. Germans made another attack under gas 3 kinds of which were identified (1) Chlorine (2) Formalin + (3) a sweet smelling gas which produced coma without affecting breathing + gave the breath + clothing an odour resembling Pear drops + [illegible] The Chlorine produced great irritation of eyes + [illegible] + the Formalin irritation of the eyes, [illegible] The gas attack was persisted in for 4 to 4½ hours + was over at HOOGE GRAAF.	

(73989) W4141—463. 400,000. 9/14. H.&J.Ltd. Forms/C. 2118/10.

10

Instructions regarding War Diaries and Intelligence Summaries are contained in F. S. Regs., Part II. and the Staff Manual respectively. Title pages will be prepared in manuscript.

WAR DIARY
or
INTELLIGENCE SUMMARY.

(Erase heading not required.)

Army Form C. 2118.

Hour, Date, Place	Summary of Events and Information	Remarks and references to Appendices
1915 May 24th	Admitted wounded 260 including [illegible] 2/Lieut. MARDEN. T.O. 1/Welch; Capt. x RAINE. A.J. 9/D.L.I.; " TINLEY. M. RAMC attd. 2/North[illegible] R.F.A.; Lieut. x HEADS. J.E.B. 9/D.L.I.; Lieut. CARPENTER. F.C.M. 8/ "; " PILTER. C. 15/Hussars; " CLAYTON. C.P. 3/Welsh attd. 1/Welch; 2/Lieut. x INNES. J.D. 9/D.L.I.; 2/ " x JONES. L. 2/E. Surrey; " x FOX. H.G. 2/Bucks; " KILKENNY. E.C.R. R.F.A.	
	Gas asphyxiation 218 x	
	Sick 43 including Capt. ROBINSON. H.F.N. R.F.A.	
	Transferred to Clearing H. 507 Discharged to Duty 29. Died 1	
25th	Gas attack was repeated & appeared to demoralise a good many men – a large number came in who were so slightly if at all affected that they were not admitted, but sent back to duty without any entry being made in the A&D Book.	
	Abdominal & Chest cases were retained & sent to the 'B' Section Hospital at the School in order to treat them & avoid the disturbance of the journey to BAILLEUL until they were considered safe. They were kept without anything by the mouth for 5 days. Given continuous saline Rectal injections or subcutaneous saline if much shocked & usually Pituitary Extract hypodermically. 30 such cases are now in this Hospital.	

(73989) W4141—463. 400,000. 9/14. H.&J.Ltd. Forms/C. 2118/10.

Instructions regarding War Diaries and Intelligence Summaries are contained in F. S. Regs., Part II. and the Staff Manual respectively. Title pages will be prepared in manuscript.

WAR DIARY
or
INTELLIGENCE SUMMARY.
(*Erase heading not required.*)

Army Form C. 2118.

11

Hour, Date, Place	Summary of Events and Information	Remarks and references to Appendices
1915 May 23rd	Very bad gas cases with symptoms of lung & mucous irritation were treated with inhalation of [illegible] solution of Sodium Carbonate under an improvised tent consisting of ground sheets. The vapour being pumped under it by means of a continuous spray. The patients expressed relief & many obviously improved. 3 very badly asphyxiated cases died in spite of all treatment & P.M. showed marked Broncho-pneumonia.	
	Admitted wounded 534 } including Major TAYLOR. W.F. 6/D.L.I.	
	for asphyxiated 288 } x Capt. x GRAHAM A. 4/Yorkshire	
	RAYMOND-GREEN. W. 9th Lancers	
	" Lieut. x TURNBULL. J.W.F. 8/D.L.I.	
	x GATHERALL. R.O. 9/ "	
	" HOLDSWORTH. H.B. 8/ "	
	" BROWN. F.D. 5/ "	
	" PARRY. L.A.R. 3/R. Fus	
	" SALIER. E.L. 3/North'd Fus	attd 2/North'd Fus
	" BUCKLE. D.F.C. 3/ "	
	" COOPER. A.P. 3/North'd	R.F.A.
	" JONES. S.L. P.P.C.L.I.	
	2/Lieut. LAIRD. J.D. 3/R. Fus	
	" PERSSE. H.W. 3/ "	
	" VAUGHAN. J.M. 1/Welsh	
	" BAGGALLAY. G.T. 1/ "	
	" LUNN. P.R. 1/ "	
	" MUNRO. H. 4/Yorkshire	
	" JONES. E.E. 1/Welsh	
	" DAVID. A.E.Y. 3/S.W. Bords	attd 2/Buffs
	" GARNON-WILLIAMS. A. RAMC	attd 1/R.I.[illegible]
	Sick 76 including Capt. HESLOP. H.L.	
	Lieut. SARGENT. L.C. 2/Buffs	
	2/Lieut. STEGGALL. G.E.A. 2/ "	
	Transferred to Clearing H. 746	
	Discharged to duty 29 Died 16 including 3 from gas asphyxiation.	

(73989) W4141—463. 400,000. 9/14. H.&J.Ltd. Forms/C. 2118/10.

12

WAR DIARY
or
INTELLIGENCE SUMMARY.
(Erase heading not required.)

Army Form C. 2118.

Instructions regarding War Diaries and Intelligence Summaries are contained in F. S. Regs., Part II. and the Staff Manual respectively. Title pages will be prepared in manuscript.

Hour, Date, Place	Summary of Events and Information	Remarks and references to Appendices
1915		
May 25th	Bearers & Motor ambulances under Lieut WOOTTON proceeded at 9 pm to White Chateau POTIJZE & cleared the Aid Posts there & were joined there at 1 am by our Asylum at YPRES. & were joined there at 1 am by our Horse ambulances in order to clear the Asylum to C. Casualty Hospital.	
26th	Admitted wounded 186 } including Brig. General PEREIRA C.E. 85th Brigade gas asphyxiated 16 } Capt. NASON E.R. 2/Cheshires LAWRENCE E.G.E. 4/E. Yorks Lieut HILL-WORKMAN J. 2/R. Scots LYON M.F. 2/ " " 2/Lieut TURNER N.H. 3rd Hussars " DART L.V. 1/Welch " JONES B.G.D. 1/ " " FREEMAN C.R. 2/North'd Fus. Sick 61 including Capt. MAIL M.E. 7/A. & S.H. " RAWES L. RAMC 84th (2nd London) Field Amb. Transferred to Clearing H. 347 Discharged to duty 7. Died 4.	
27th	Every Motor Ambulance rendezvoused at Asylum YPRES at 4 am. & evacuated wounded to C. C. Stn. Admitted wounded 60 } including Lieut CLARKE A.F. 5/Yorkshires gas asphyxiated 6 } Sick 26 Transferred to Clearing H. 91. Discharged to Duty 18.	

13

Instructions regarding War Diaries and Intelligence Summaries are contained in F. S. Regs., Part II. and the Staff Manual respectively. Title pages will be prepared in manuscript.

WAR DIARY
or
INTELLIGENCE SUMMARY.
(Erase heading not required.)

Army Form C. 2118.

Hour, Date, Place	Summary of Events and Information	Remarks and references to Appendices
1915 May 28th	Admitted wounded 51 including Capt. S.O. BAXTER 9/D.L.I. [illegible] 13	
	Sick 62	
	Transferred to Clearing H. 86 Discharged to Duty 18	
29th	5 Motor Ambulances cleared Asylum YPRES to C. Section [illegible] at 4 am	
	Ordered to move unit to HERZEELE on 31st. Sent an advance party under Capt. POTTER to arrange Billets & Hospital & clean same.	
	Admitted wounded 48	
	Sick 46 including Major SPAIN. J. 7/D.L.I. Lieut. STEVENS C.F.B. 2/1 K.O.R.L.	
	Transferred to Clearing H. 110 Discharged to Duty 25 Died 2	
30th	5 Motor Ambulances proceeded at 4 am to Asylum YPRES & evacuated wounded to C. Section	
	Admitted wounded 54	
	Sick 52 including 2/Lieut NEWELL T.S. 3/Cheshires attached 2/Cheshires 2/Lieut SOMERSET W.H.S. 3/Monmouths	
	Transferred to Clearing H. 65	
	Discharged to Duty 13.	

(73989) W4141—463. 400,000. 9/14. H.&J.Ltd. Forms/C. 2118/10.

14

Instructions regarding War Diaries and Intelligence Summaries are contained in F. S. Regs., Part II. and the Staff Manual respectively. Title pages will be prepared in manuscript.

WAR DIARY
or
INTELLIGENCE SUMMARY.

(Erase heading not required.)

Army Form C. 2118.

Hour, Date, Place	Summary of Events and Information	Remarks and references to Appendices
1915		
May 30th	No 3250 Pte BIGGS G.W. " 3254 " BRUFORD W.F. " 3257 " JARRETT W.J " 3258 " STUBBS F.H. " 3269 " WEST A.H. } proceeded to BAILLEUL to report to the R.T.O. for transfer to their original unit the 3rd Home Counties Field Ambulance – T.F.	
31st	2 Motor Ambulances proceeded at 4 am to join the Motor Convoy at the Asylum YPRES & evacuate wounded to C. Section	
	Admitted wounded 12 gas asphyxiated 1 Sick 62 including Lieut STOWELL W.R. R.E.	
	Transferred to Clearing H. 74 discharged to Duty 36.	
	At 10 am the unit moved off to HERZEELE after handing over the Hospital & several abdominal cases not fit for transfer, to the 7th Field Ambulance	
	At HERZEELE we opened up a Hospital in a small Chateau for 30 cases in beds & for 180 in 48 Bell & 3 operating tents in a field behind the Chateau.	
	The personnel bivouacing.	
	We are to take over charge of the 84th Brigade area & their sick while in rest billets here.	

(73989) W4141—463. 400,000. 9/14. H.&J.Ltd. Forms/C. 2118/10.

15

Instructions regarding War Diaries and Intelligence Summaries are contained in F. S. Regs., Part II. and the Staff Manual respectively. Title pages will be prepared in manuscript.

WAR DIARY
or
INTELLIGENCE SUMMARY.
(Erase heading not required.)

Army Form C. 2118.

Hour, Date, Place	Summary of Events and Information	Remarks and references to Appendices
1915		
May 31st	The classification of wounds treated & total deaths in the Field Ambulance for the month of May is as shown in the accompanying Chart Appendix I	See Appendix I
	Total admissions for May: Sick 1099 (including shell concussion, burns, sprains & contusions); Wounded 2322; Gas asphyxiated 541; total 3962	
	& Total since Feb 3rd: Sick 4281; Wounded 5002; Gassed 567; total 9850	
		[illegible] Lt Col O.C. 88th (3rd London) Field Ambulance

(73989) W4141—463. 400,000. 9/14. H.&J.Ltd. Forms/C. 2118/10.

APPENDIX. I

N.B. THE FIGURES FOR FRACTURES. ARE IN EVERY CASE INCLUDED IN THOSE OF THE PART INJURED.

CLASSIFICATION of WOUNDED

ADMITTED TO 85TH FIELD AMBLCE DURING THE MONTH OF MAY 1915.

	WOUNDS OF HEAD.				NECK	CHEST	ABDOMEN	BACK			ARMS						LEGS.							TOTAL. NO. DEATH	TOTAL NO WOUNDS.
	SCALP	SKULL	FACE	JAW				BACK	SHLDRS	BUTTKS	HUMERUS	fract.	FOREARM.	fract.	HAND	FINGER	THIGH	fract.	KNEE	LOWER LEG	fract.	ANCLE	FOOT.		
GUNSHOT	47	36 1	34	2	15	35	24 8	32 1	49 1	31 1	57	(2)	76	(9)	60	28	89 1	(7)	39	70	(6)	12	50	13	786
SHELL	90	82 1	70	10	33	48 1	66 18	105 4	100 1	59	118 2	(12)	68	(5)	64	26	161	(12)	55	179 4	(21)	25	68	31	1427
GRENADE OR MORTAR			1		1				2				1		2	1									8
TOTALS.	137	118 2	105	12.	49	83 1	90 26	137 5	151 2	90	175 2	(14)	145	(14)	126	55	250 1	(19)	94	249 4	(26)	37	118	44	2221

No 85. 7 a.

May 1915

28 Division

121/6243

121/6243

June '15

85th Field Ambulance

Vol VI

Instructions regarding War Diaries and Intelligence Summaries are contained in F. S. Regs., Part II. and the Staff Manual respectively. Title pages will be prepared in manuscript.

WAR DIARY
or
INTELLIGENCE SUMMARY.
(Erase heading not required.)

Army Form C. 2118.

1

Hour, Date, Place	Summary of Events and Information	Remarks and references to Appendices
1915		
June 1st	Admitted Sick 19 including Capt. EDWARDS. A.M. 7/Lancashire Lieut. WILLIAMS. L.O. 2/ "	Major E.N. WAGGETT Capt. H.A.T. FAIRBANK " R.M. VICK Lieut. TAYLOR. J. " Q.M. P.S. BAYNES proceeded on 5 days leave to England.
	Transferred to Clearing H. 22 discharged to duty 8	
2nd	Admitted Sick 15 discharged to duty 9.	
3rd	Admitted Sick 12 including Lieut. ALLPRESS. H.G. 1/Lancashire	
	Transferred to Clearing H. 4 discharged to duty 6	
	~~Without exception~~ all the Regimental M.Os being Temporary Lieutenants without previous experience of Camp & Billet Sanitation, some difficulty was experienced at first in getting sanitary measures adopted for the protection of food & water from contamination by means of flies, which are a great nuisance here. However by means of personal instruction in the methods of constructing & using Incinerators, urine pits, Soakage pits, grease traps, Swill tubs, &c & in keeping them clean & free from flies, & further in organizing the men which in billets into messes & so supervising the food after issue, it has been possible already to greatly reduce the Fly trouble &	

(73989) W4141—463. 400,000. 9/14. H.&J.Ltd. Forms/C. 2118/10.

Instructions regarding War Diaries and Intelligence Summaries are contained in F. S. Regs., Part II. and the Staff Manual respectively. Title pages will be prepared in manuscript.

2

WAR DIARY
or
INTELLIGENCE SUMMARY.
(Erase heading not required.)

Army Form C. 2118.

Hour, Date, Place	Summary of Events and Information	Remarks and references to Appendices
1915		
June 2?	the liability to intestinal diseases. Some trouble was given by the CO's of several units putting difficulties in the way of the suggested feeding arrangement, especially on account of the scarcity of wood with which to make tables & seats. This difficulty was surmounted however by showing them the example of a Trench Table as standing in our own camp. Another difficulty which had to be overcome was the objection of CO's to [illegible] the [illegible] placed over the latrines to ensure the efficient covering of faeces & paper with earth. It is hoped that by these various means the incidence of sickness amongst the troops of the Brigade will be kept low.	
	No 390. Pte KING W " 389 " BRAMHALL. BVS. " 284 " GIBSON. L.V " 311 " SHARPE. H.R " 425 " JACQUES. C.H " 452 " KING. N " 319 " BUNYARD. T " 321 " SCOTT. J.L " 160 Corpl BAWTREE. A.L. } These men joined from ROUEN as reinforcements & were taken on the strength of the unit.	
	" 020613. Pte KENDAL. E joined from Mechanical Transport A.S.C. & is taken on the strength attached.	
	Lieut. R.E. BARNSLEY returned to duty from England.	

(73989) W4141—463. 400,000. 9/14. H.&J.Ltd. Forms/C. 2118/10.

Instructions regarding War Diaries and Intelligence Summaries are contained in F. S. Regs., Part II. and the Staff Manual respectively. Title pages will be prepared in manuscript.

3/

WAR DIARY
or
INTELLIGENCE SUMMARY.
(Erase heading not required.)

Army Form C. 2118.

Hour, Date, Place	Summary of Events and Information	Remarks and references to Appendices
1915		
June 4th	Admitted Sick 14 Wounded 2 Gas asphyxiated 1 Transferred to Clearing H. 2 Discharged to duty 8 The G.O.C. Lt General BULFIN inspected the Hospital	
5th	Admitted Sick 10 Transferred to Clearing H. 7 Discharged to duty 9. Daily Gas Respirator parades commenced to familiarise the personnel with their use	
6th	Admitted Sick 15 Wounded 1 Discharged to duty 9. 10 N.C.O's & men proceeded to England on 5 days leave the first leave granted since our landing.	
7th	Admitted Sick 26 including Capt. BARTON, G.R. 2/Hampshires Lieut. GROVES, E.J. 2/" 2/Lieut PARSONS, J.C. 1/Suffolk Transferred to Clearing H. 2 Discharged to Duty 5	

Instructions regarding War Diaries and Intelligence Summaries are contained in F. S. Regs., Part II. and the Staff Manual respectively. Title pages will be prepared in manuscript.

4

WAR DIARY
or
INTELLIGENCE SUMMARY.
(Erase heading not required.)

Army Form C. 2118.

Hour, Date, Place	Summary of Events and Information	Remarks and references to Appendices
1915		
June 8th	Capt. POTTER. B.E., Lieut. ROBBINS F.H., TAYLOR J, SMITH K.V } Proceeded on 5 days leave to England	
	Admitted Sick 25, Wounded 1 — Discharged to Duty 10	
9th	Admitted Sick 20 — Discharged to Duty 12	1 proceeded on 5 days leave to England.
	Transferred to Clearing H. 7	
10th	Appointed Lieut. R.E. BARNSLEY as officer responsible for arranging diets for patients in Hospital, as the G.O.C. wishes us to run the unit on lines of a Stationary Hospital while in the resting area.	
	Wire rims ordered to be removed from F.S. Caps on account of visibility of the stiff disc - the top of the cap as seen from above.	
	Admitted Sick 10 - including Capt. EDWARDS. A. 1/Munsters, Wounded 3, Gas Asphyxiated 1 — Discharged to Duty 13	
11th	Admitted Sick 30 including Capt. DILLON. E.F.G. Brigade Major 84th Brigade, Gas Asphyxiated 1	
	Transferred to Clearing H. 1 — Discharged to Duty 3	

(73989) W4141—463. 400,000. 9/14. H.&J.Ltd. Forms/C. 2118/10.

Instructions regarding War Diaries and Intelligence Summaries are contained in F. S. Regs., Part II. and the Staff Manual respectively. Title pages will be prepared in manuscript.

WAR DIARY
or
INTELLIGENCE SUMMARY.
(*Erase heading not required.*)

Army Form C. 2118.

Hour, Date, Place	Summary of Events and Information	Remarks and references to Appendices
1915		
June 12th	Admitted sick 4. Discharged to duty 1	
13th	C Section under Capt. VICK & Lieut. ROBBINS took over the Chateau MONT NOIR & the officers convalescent Rest Station there & the officers [illegible] there were transferred to our A.D. Books from 42nd Field Ambulance	
	Admitted sick 27 including Major HARRISON. E.J. 6/Lincolns	
	Capts. BARTHOLOMEW. G. 1/Gordons attached 5/K.S.L.I.	
	" AMERY. W.M. C.F. attached [illegible]	
	" CHURTON. W.A.V. 5/[illegible]	
	Lieuts. HOPE-HALL. E.C. 9/London	
	" LLOYD. R. RAMC attached 2/[illegible]	
	" BARRY. J.H. R.E.	
	" CHESTER. C.C.	
	" CLARKE. R.C. 5/KSLI	
	2/Lieut. GAULTER. C.V. 5/KORL	
	" GILLESPIE. R. 2/KOSB	
	" CATTLEY. E. 4/N. Staffs attached 2/KOSB	
	" McLEAN. A.N. 1/Wilts	
	" TORRANCE 2/[illegible]	
	" DUNCAN. L. 9/London	
	Transferred to Clearing H. 1. Discharged to duty 12.	
14th	Admitted sick 5	
	for asphyxiation 1	
	Transferred to Clearing H. 15.	
	Transferred to convalescent Rest Station MONT des CATS 101. Discharged to duty 16.	

(73989) W4141—463. 400,000. 9/14. H.&J.Ltd. Forms/C. 2118/10.

Army Form C. 2118.

Instructions regarding War Diaries and Intelligence Summaries are contained in F. S. Regs., Part II. and the Staff Manual respectively. Title pages will be prepared in manuscript.

WAR DIARY
or
INTELLIGENCE SUMMARY.
(Erase heading not required.)

6

Hour, Date, Place	Summary of Events and Information	Remarks and references to Appendices
1915		
June 14th	Moved A & B Sections to WESTOUTRE after evacuating HERZEELE Hospital. & took over the Convent-School as Hospital for serious cases of sick & a neighbouring field in which we pitched [illegible] Bell Tents & 3 [illegible] Tents for accommodation of 180 sick as a Convalescent Rest Camp. B Section opened & took over charge of the Hospital.	
15th	Admitted sick 14. including 2/Lieut GREEN H.J. 1/Dorsets.	
16th	Moved the personnel out of Billets into Bivouac. & Officers into Tents. Admitted sick 5. Discharged to duty 5.	
17th	Admitted sick 6. including Capt. SNEPP R.N.E. 1/Norfolks, Lieut BAINBRIDGE-BELL [illegible] 9/Roy [illegible] attd [illegible]	
	Transferred to Clearing P. 1	
18th	Admitted sick 16 including Capt. BOSANQUET O.P. 1/DCLI, 2/Lieut DUNN J.E. 2/Mons, ESSEX A.C. 1/Y&L, MAPPIN S.A. 4/Warwicks attd 2/Cheshires, SLOMAN A.J. 2/[illegible]. Wounded 2	
19th	Admitted sick 7 including Lieut SANDERS G.J. 4/[illegible] attd [illegible], 2/Lieut WILLIAMS E.M. 3/[illegible], De SALIS J.J. 8/ " . Discharged to duty 3.	
	Discharged to duty 4.	

Instructions regarding War Diaries and Intelligence Summaries are contained in F. S. Regs., Part II. and the Staff Manual respectively. Title pages will be prepared in manuscript.

7.

WAR DIARY
or
INTELLIGENCE SUMMARY.
(Erase heading not required.)

Army Form C. 2118.

Hour, Date, Place	Summary of Events and Information	Remarks and references to Appendices
1915		
June 20th	Admitted Sick 3 including Capt. BLEST. M.A. 1/ Middlesex; Lieut. GARRETT. H.F.B. 2/ Surreys	
	Transferred to Clearing Stn. 3 discharged to duty 6.	
21st	Pte BARRATT. A.K. developed acute Septicaemia, result of a fly bite on side of bridge of nose - with symptoms also of thrombosis of Cavernous Sinus. Staphylococcus only organism grown from culture of discharge from the wound. He thinks he was bitten while at HERZEELE.	
	Admitted Sick 40 discharged to duty 1.	
22nd	Admitted Sick 32 including Lieut. MATTHEWS. J.B. RAMC attd 1/ D.C.L.I.; 2/Lieut. RAWLINGS. J.H. 2/ K.O.S.B.; Lt. & QM. PEIRCE. A.E. 1/ Bedfords	
	Transferred to Clearing Stn 1 discharged to duty 2.	
23rd	Pte BARRATT died - Post mortem. Cavernous Sinuses were blocked with purulent clot. & localised meningitis.	
	Admitted Sick 13 discharged to duty 3. died 1.	
24th	QM Sergt. CANHAM. H.W.H. promoted to Warrant Officer Class II	
	Admitted Sick 6 including Lieut. SAYWELL. J.R. A.S.C.; 2/Lieut. BUCKLEY. E.K. 6/ Liverpool	
	Wounded 1	
	7 discharged to duty 9.	

(73989) W4141—463. 400,000. 9/14. H.&J.Ltd. Forms/C. 2118/10.

Instructions regarding War Diaries and Intelligence Summaries are contained in F. S. Regs., Part II. and the Staff Manual respectively. Title pages will be prepared in manuscript.

8

WAR DIARY
or
INTELLIGENCE SUMMARY.
(Erase heading not required.)

Army Form C. 2118.

Hour, Date, Place	Summary of Events and Information	Remarks and references to Appendices
1915 June 25th	Lieut. K.V. SMITH. reported for duty off sick leave in England.	
	Admitted Sick 45. including Lieut. COLEY. S.C. 1/A.C.C.S.	
	" HODGE. W.L. RAMC	
	2/Lieut. LEIGH. H.B. 5/Cheshire	
	Wounded 1 → " BURTON. R.W. 1/5 Surrey	
	46 " WYMAN. B. 5/Cheshire	
	Transferred to Clearing H. 1 Discharged to Duty 23.	
26th	No 199 Pte COTTAM. T.M. detailed to be attached to office of ADMS for course of instruction in Hd Quarters office routine.	
	Admitted Sick 84 including Lieut SEWELL. V.C. 1/R.W. Kent	
	" RASHLEY. H.P. 9/London	
	" MORTIMER. R.H. RAMC attd 2/[illegible]	
	2/Lieut DISLEY-HERBERT. A. 9/London	
	Transferred to Clearing H. 3 Discharged to Duty 1	
27th	Admitted Sick 40 including Capt. ADAMSON. A.G. 3/4 Staffords attached 2/[illegible]	
	Lieut WORMINGTON. W.T. 1/Cheshire	
	" HEALD. T.L.C. 5/ "	
	Transferred to Clearing H. 2 Discharged to Duty 20.	

(73989) W4141—463. 400,000. 9/14. H.&J.Ltd. Forms/C. 2118/10.

Army Form C. 2118.

WAR DIARY
or
INTELLIGENCE SUMMARY.
(Erase heading not required.)

Instructions regarding War Diaries and Intelligence Summaries are contained in F. S. Regs., Part II. and the Staff Manual respectively. Title pages will be prepared in manuscript.

9

Hour, Date, Place	Summary of Events and Information	Remarks and references to Appendices
1915		
June 28th	Admitted sick 7 including Capt. LAMPREY. J.C. 2/E. Yorks; Major WAINWRIGHT R. 6/Liverpools; 2/Lieut FULLER. W.R. 1/Dorsets; " HUSKENS. C.J. 2/E. Surrey; " BAKER. C.H. 3/D.L.I. attd 2/North Lan.	
	Transferred to Clearing H. 2 Discharged to Duty 2	
29th	Admitted Sick 9 including Lieut SANDILANDS. R.D. 2/Buffs	
	Transferred to Clearing H 1 Discharged to Duty 8.	
30th	Admitted Sick 27, wounded 1 including 2/Lieut ROYSTON. J.W. 6/Liverpools	
	Transferred to Clearing H 3 Discharged to Duty 25.	
	By the system adopted in the 28th Division of retaining sick & wounded ~~[illegible]~~ likely to be fit for duty in a few days, or after a further 14 days in a Convalescent Rest Station instead of evacuating them straight away to Clearing Hospital, an enormous wastage has been prevented to the Division.	
	Driver TREE wounded in face & neck by Shrapnel at DICKEBUSCH & evacuated to Clearing H.	

10

Instructions regarding War Diaries and Intelligence Summaries are contained in F. S. Regs., Part II. and the Staff Manual respectively. Title pages will be prepared in manuscript.

WAR DIARY
or
INTELLIGENCE SUMMARY.
(Erase heading not required.)

Army Form C. 2118.

Hour, Date, Place	Summary of Events and Information	Remarks and references to Appendices
1915 June 20th	Classification of wounded admitted during the month of June	

	HEAD	HAND	BUTTOCKS	LEG	TOTALS
GUNSHOT	1	2			3
SHELL	1				1
GRENADE or MORTAR	2	3	1	1	7
TOTAL	4	5	1	1	11

Total DEATHS 1

Total Admissions for June		Total since Feb 3rd	
Sick	583	Sick	4864
Wounded	11	Wounded	5013
Gas asphyxiation	7	Gassed	574
	601		10451

[illegible] Lt Col
O.C. 85th (3rd London) Field Ambulance

28th Division

121/6243.

121/6243

July '15

85th Field Ambulance

Vol VII.

Instructions regarding War Diaries and Intelligence Summaries are contained in F. S. Regs., Part II. and the Staff Manual respectively. Title pages will be prepared in manuscript.

WAR DIARY
or
INTELLIGENCE SUMMARY.
(Erase heading not required.)

Army Form C. 2118.

Hour, Date, Place	Summary of Events and Information	Remarks and references to Appendices
1915 July 1st	Admitted Sick 5 including Capt. GOLDINGHAM. D.D. 3/Middlesex, 2/Lieut. ADDERLEY. A.K. 1/Cheshire, " THORNWILL J.H.H. R.F.A.	
	Transferred to Clearing H. 3 Discharged to Duty 7.	
2nd	Admitted Sick 5 including Capt. HEPBURN. 3/Roy. Fus., 2/Lieut. GLENDENNING. H.W. 5/Cheshire	
	Transferred to Clearing H. 5 Discharged to Duty 13.	
3rd	Admitted Sick 10 including 2/Lieut. HARDING G.P. 1/Cheshire	
	Transferred to Clearing H. 1 Discharged to Duty 11	
4th	Admitted Sick 19 including Lieut. GRIFFITHS. E.W. RAMC attd. 31st Bgd R.F.A., 2/Lieut. TAYLOR. D.E.D. 3/Roy. Fus.	
	Transferred to Clearing H. 3 Discharged to Duty 19.	
5th	Admitted Sick 29 including Lt. Col. MARTIN. R.E. 4/Leinster, 2/Lieut. CAYLEY. C. 1/Monmouths	
	Transferred to Clearing H. 2 Discharged to Duty 23.	
6th	Admitted Sick 16 including 2/Lieut. RONALDSON-CLARK. C.G. R.F.A. attd. R.F.C., CUNNINGHAM. E.M. 3/Somerset L.I. attd. 2/Duke of Wellington's	
	Wounded 1 — 2/Lieut. CARPENTER. A.E. 1/Roy. W. Kent	
	Transferred to Clearing H. 2 Discharged to Duty 6.	

2

Instructions regarding War Diaries and Intelligence Summaries are contained in F. S. Regs., Part II. and the Staff Manual respectively. Title pages will be prepared in manuscript.

WAR DIARY
or
INTELLIGENCE SUMMARY.
(Erase heading not required.)

Army Form C. 2118.

Hour, Date, Place	Summary of Events and Information	Remarks and references to Appendices
1915 July 7th	Admitted Sick 6 including Lt Col. WILLIAMS. S.G. 1/Dorsets	
	Lieut. COOPER. L.H. 1/Roy W. Kent	
	" GODDING. H.C. R.A.M.C. attd 2/KORL	
	" BAMBRIDGE. W.J. A.V.C	
	2/Lieut TAYLOR. B.M. 1/A.C.L.I.	
	Wounded 1	
	Transferred to Clearing H. 3 Discharged to Duty 16	
8th	Ordered to close our Convalescent Rest Camp & open up & work as a Field Ambulance to serve the area & Reg. aid Posts of the 83rd Brigade. C Section continuing to run the Convalescent Rest Station for Officers at MONT NOIR. Patients in Hospital not likely to be fit in 14 days were transferred to Clearing H. BAILLEUL. Patients fit for duty were Discharged – & those likely to be fit in 14 days were transferred to the Convalescent Rest Camp opened up at BOESCHEPE by the 86th Field Ambulance	
	Admitted Sick 11 including Capt. TOLLEMACHE. H.D.M. 4/Bedfords attd Yorks	
	" WILLIAMS. L.M. 3/Middlesex	
	Lieut FRERE. B.L.S 1/Bedfords	
	" LLOYD. K 9/London	
	" GOSTLING. B.W 3/Roy. Fus	
	2/Lieut TUDOR-BENNETT. C 1/Roy. W. Kent	
	Transferred to Clearing H. 11	
	Discharged to Duty 54	

3

Instructions regarding War Diaries and Intelligence Summaries are contained in F. S. Regs., Part II. and the Staff Manual respectively. Title pages will be prepared in manuscript.

WAR DIARY
or
INTELLIGENCE SUMMARY.
(Erase heading not required.)

Army Form C. 2118.

Hour, Date, Place	Summary of Events and Information	Remarks and references to Appendices
1915 July 9th	Admitted Sick 4 including Major SINCLAIR-THOMPSON. G.A.L.	1/Suffolks
	Lieut. McCLELLAND. N.P.	3/Roy. W. Kent attd 1/R.W.K.
	" BARTON. P.G.	3/Roy. Fus.
	2/Lieut. FULCHER. R.E.J.	1/Roy. W. Kent.
	Transferred to Clearing Stn 5 Discharged to Duty 26.	
10th	Admitted Sick 18 including Lt Col. SHARPE. W.S. R.A.M.C.T. 84th (2nd London) Fd Amb	
	Major ROCHE. B.R.	1/Bedford
	Capt. RUSSELL. E.G.	1/Roy. W. Kent.
	Lieut. RUSSELL-JONES. W.F.	9/London
	" GURDON. J	2/E. Surrey
	Transferred to Clearing Stn 3 " to Conv. Rest Camp 3 Discharged to Duty 9.	
11th	Reconnoitred the front about VERSTRAAT accompanied by 83rd Brigade to locate tracks for Bearers to use for getting back wounded from Reg. Aid Post to Advanced Dressing Station & ambulances.	
	Admitted Sick 27 including Major ELLIS. R.H. 2/1 C.O.Y.H. Lieut. HARWOOD L.A. RAMCT 84th (2nd London) Fd Amb	
	Transferred to Clearing Stn 5 " to Conv. Rest Camp 33 Discharged to Duty 28	

Instructions regarding War Diaries and Intelligence Summaries are contained in F. S. Regs., Part II. and the Staff Manual respectively. Title pages will be prepared in manuscript.

4

WAR DIARY
or
INTELLIGENCE SUMMARY.
(Erase heading not required.)

Army Form C. 2118.

Hour, Date, Place	Summary of Events and Information	Remarks and references to Appendices
1915		
July 12th	Made further reconnaissance of ground up to Ry and Post with view to determining alternative routes back from there.	
	Admitted Sick 23 including Lieut. STUDDERT R.H. RFA, 2/Lieut SMITH W.J. 1/Dorsets	
	Transferred to Clearing H. 5, to Conval. Rest Camp 3, Discharged to Duty 15	
13th	Despatched S/Sgt. CASWELL & 8 Bearers & two cyclists to establish an Advanced Dressing Station in cellar of a Farm in N.9.a.8.1 Sheet 28 (YPRES), to deal with any cases during the day & up to which it would be possible to bring motor ambulances during daylight.	
	Admitted Sick 11 including Major BORRETT O.G. 2/KORL, Lieut WORMALD L.G. RFA, " BRINK J.H. ", 2/Lieut COLE L.S. 2/Cheshire	
	Transferred to Clearing H. 5, to Conval. Rest Camp 21, Discharged to Duty 9	

(73989) W4141—463. 400,000. 9/14. H.&J.Ltd. Forms/C. 2118/10.

5

WAR DIARY
or
INTELLIGENCE SUMMARY.
(Erase heading not required.)

Army Form C. 2118.

Instructions regarding War Diaries and Intelligence Summaries are contained in F. S. Regs., Part II. and the Staff Manual respectively. Title pages will be prepared in manuscript.

Hour, Date, Place	Summary of Events and Information	Remarks and references to Appendices
1915 July 14th	Admitted Sick 5 including Lieut SIDEBOTHAM. E.M. 1/Cheshire, 2/Lieut FRASER. W.H. 2/Monmouth, 2nd Col. ROBERTS. A.S. 3/Roy Fus	
	Transferred to Clearing Hosp. 4	
	" to Convalescent Camp 12 Discharged to duty 5	
15th	Ordered to ~~open~~ take over the Hospital LOCRE from the 2/3rd Northumbrian Field Ambulance 50th (Northumbrian) Division & to open up Hospital there for reception of wounded from 84th Brigade area opposite KEMMEL. The 85th Field Ambulance to evacuate from the 83rd Brigade area. A Section to open up at LOCRE. [illegible] detailed B Section & Hd. Quarters remains at WESTOUTRE to take in sick & C Section remains at MONT NOIR	
	Withdrawn party from advanced Dressing Station at VERSTRAAT	
	Admitted Sick 34 including Capt. TEALL. G.H. 6/Liverpool; Lieut PERKINS. W.V. 5/Roy. W. Surrey; " CHUBB. P.A. 2/KOYLI; 2/Lieut BATES. B.A. 3/Y&L; " PULLEN. F.J. 1/Welsh; " ELLISON. A.J. 1/Y&L; " COLES. J.L. 1/ "; " BOUCHER. E.G. 2/Monmouth	
	Transferred to Clearing Hosp 1	
	Discharged to duty 13.	

(73989) W4141—463. 400,000. 9/14. H.&J.Ltd. Forms/C. 2118/10.

Army Form C. 2118

Instructions regarding War Diaries and Intelligence Summaries are contained in F. S. Regs., Part II. and the Staff Manual respectively. Title Pages will be prepared in manuscript.

6

WAR DIARY
or
INTELLIGENCE SUMMARY

(Erase heading not required.)

Place	Date	Hour	Summary of Events and Information	Remarks and references to Appendices
1915	July	16th	Went over to LOCRE to arrange to take over the Hospital tomorrow afternoon. Were proceeded to locate the Regt' aid posts of the [illegible] Brigade [illegible] by a communication trench 1½ miles long one of which is from LINDENHOEK by a [illegible] The aid posts being in 'Dug outs' at a [illegible] called KINGSWAY & REGENT ST about 350 yards behind the fire trench of the trench named PALL MALL.	
			Admitted Sick 12 including Major TOKE R.T. 1/Welsh; 2/Lieut. HUGHES. P.R. RFA; " MILNER. S.A. 2/KORL.	
			Wounded 1	
			Transferred to Clearing H. 2	
			" Conval.t Rest Camp 4	
			Discharged to duty 6.	
"		17th	A Section complete, less C.O. Serjt-Major & Serjt. PRIOR (Ord. room Clerk) proceeded under Capt. FAIRBANK, Lieut. BARNSLEY & Lieut. SMITH to LOCRE & opened up as Dressing Station & Hospital to serve 84th Brigade area.	
			Admitted Sick 14 including Lieut. FORSYTH. A. 9/London	
			Wounded 2	
			Gas Asphyxiated 1	
			Transferred to Clearing H. 4	
			" " Conval.t Rest Camp 4	
			Discharged to Duty 7.	

1875 Wt. W593/826 1,000,000 4/15 J.B.C. & A. A.D.S.S./Forms/C. 2118.

Instructions regarding War Diaries and Intelligence Summaries are contained in F. S. Regs., Part II. and the Staff Manual respectively. Title Pages will be prepared in manuscript.

7

WAR DIARY
or
INTELLIGENCE SUMMARY
(Erase heading not required.)

Army Form C. 2118

Place	Date	Hour	Summary of Events and Information	Remarks and references to Appendices
1915	July	18th	Admitted Sick 37 including Lieut HAIG D. RAMC att/ [illegible]; 2/Lieut BURTONCEY RFA.	
			Transferred to Clearing H. 2; " Conval. Rest Camp 0. Discharged to duty 6	
		19th	Admitted Sick 57 including Capt. STEEL O.W.W 3/Monmouths; Lieut HART C.L. 2/S. Wales Borderers; 2/Lieut DOWNEY W.R. 2/ "; " NEWROTH W.S 2/ "; " DAVIDSON R.J. 2/Buffs; " TAUNTON C.W. 2/Monmouths	
			Wounded 11 — 68	
			Transferred to Clearing H. 9; " Conval. Rest Camp 6. Discharged to duty 12.	
		20th	Admitted Sick 45 including Lt Col ASHTON C.G. 2/E. Surreys; 2/Lieut McGOWAN G. 5/Cheshires; " CUNNINGHAM E.M. 3/Somersets attd to 2/5th [illegible]	[illegible]
			Wounded 4 — 49	
			Transferred to Clearing H. 8; " Conval. Rest Camp 7. Discharged to duty 4.	

1875 Wt. W593/826 1,000,000 4/15 J.B.C. & A. A.D.S.S./Forms/C. 2118.

Army Form C. 2118

Instructions regarding War Diaries and Intelligence Summaries are contained in F. S. Regs., Part II. and the Staff Manual respectively. Title Pages will be prepared in manuscript.

8

WAR DIARY
or
INTELLIGENCE SUMMARY
(Erase heading not required.)

Place	Date	Hour	Summary of Events and Information	Remarks and references to Appendices
1915	July	21st	Admitted Sick 31 including Capt. WILLIAMS. L. M. 3/Middlesex Lieut. BOLSOVER. G. R.G.A. 2/Lieut. HENSON. J. 2/KORL " BLUCKE. W. S. 1/[illegible] " GREW. B. D. 2/North. Fus.	
			Wounded 2 including Capt. NICHOLSON. A. F. R.F.A. 33	
			Transferred to Clearing H. 4 Discharged to duty 38	
			" " Conval. Rest Camp 11	
		22nd	Admitted Sick 28 including Lieut. PEARSON-BELL. 6/Welch	
			Wounded 2 30	
			Transferred to Clearing H. 5	
			" " Conval. Rest Camp 19. Discharged to duty 8.	
		23rd	Admitted Sick 49. including 2/Lieut. MELLOR. W. M. 3/Roy. Fus. " MILLER-HALLETT. J. H. " "	
			Wounded 12 including 2/Lieut. WILLIAMS W. S. 6/Welch 61	
			Transferred to Clearing H. 11	
			" " Conval. Rest Camp 31 Discharged to duty 12.	

1875 Wt. W593/826 1,000,000 4/15 J.B.C. & A. A.D.S.S./Forms/C. 2118.

9

Instructions regarding War Diaries and Intelligence Summaries are contained in F. S. Regs., Part II. and the Staff Manual respectively. Title Pages will be prepared in manuscript.

WAR DIARY
or
INTELLIGENCE SUMMARY
(Erase heading not required.)

Army Form C. 2118

Place	Date	Hour	Summary of Events and Information	Remarks and references to Appendices
1915	July	24th	The 86th Field Ambulance having been detailed to take over the Hospice LOCRE. 'A' Section returned to & rejoined Head Quarters of unit at 'B' Section at WESTOUTRE from whence we will still continue to clear 88th Brigade area of wounded.	
			Admitted Sick 23	
			Wounded 4	
			27	
			Transferred to Clearing H. 11	
			" Convalt Rest Camp 13 — Discharged to Duty 3.	
			" 86th Field Amb. 20	
		25th	Awarded Pte COWELL J.P. No 34 28 days Field Punishment No 1 for disobedience to Orders (1) attempting to evade Censor (2) Commandeering a Camera (3) intending to use a Camera.	
			Admitted Sick 5 including Lieut WILSON, W.M. RAMC	
			Wounded 1	
			6	
			Transferred to Clearing H. 6 — Discharged to duty 7.	
			" Convalt Rest Camp 6	
			Sergt MARSHALL 8 men & motor equipment proceeded to Advanced Dressing Station at KEMMEL.	

1875 Wt. W593/826 1,000,000 4/15 J.B.C. & A. A.D.S.S./Forms/C. 2118.

Army Form C. 2118

WAR DIARY
or
INTELLIGENCE SUMMARY
(Erase heading not required.)

Instructions regarding War Diaries and Intelligence Summaries are contained in F. S. Regs., Part II. and the Staff Manual respectively. Title Pages will be prepared in manuscript.

10

Place	Date	Hour	Summary of Events and Information	Remarks and references to Appendices
1915	July 26th		Admitted Sick 14 Wounded 10 24 Transferred to Clearing H. 7 Discharged to duty 12. Died 1. " " Conval. Rest Camp 11	
	27th		No 59 Pte POUNDALL. W.A.L. proceeded to G.H.Q. St OMER. to undergo course of training at Cadet School BLENDECQUES. prior to taking up Commission in Infantry. Admitted Sick 8 including 2/Lieut. PROUD. W.J. 3/D.L.I. att'd 1/K.O.Y.L.I. Wounded 8 16 Transferred to Clearing H. 12 Discharged to duty 10. " " Conval. Rest Camp 11 Capt. STANTON & 8 men returned Advanced Dressing Station party.	
	28th		Admitted Sick 6 including Capt. MORRELL. J.F.B. 2/K.O.R.L. 2/Lieut. WOODYEAR. S.J.D. 2/E.Surrey " GARRETT. H.F.B. 2/. Wounded 9 15 Transferred to Clearing H. 8 Discharged to duty 26. Died 1. " " Conval. Rest Camp 26	

1875 Wt. W593/826 1,000,000 4/15 J.B.C. & A. A.D.S.S./Forms/C. 2118.

Instructions regarding War Diaries and Intelligence Summaries are contained in F. S. Regs., Part II. and the Staff Manual respectively. Title Pages will be prepared in manuscript.

11

Army Form C. 2118

WAR DIARY
or
INTELLIGENCE SUMMARY
(Erase heading not required.)

Place	Date	Hour	Summary of Events and Information	Remarks and references to Appendices
1915	July	29th	Admitted Sick 5 including Capt. ROLLS. S.P.A. 1/Dorset	
			Transferred to Clearing H. 0 Discharged to duty 3. Died 1	
			" " Conval. Rest Camp 7	
		30th	Admitted Sick 10	
			Wounded 8	
			18	
			Transferred to Clearing H. 9 Discharged to duty 3	
			" Conval. Rest Camp 1	
		31st	Admitted Sick 8	
			Wounded 2	
			10	
			Transferred to Clearing H. 2 Discharged to duty 5	
			" " Conval. Rest Camp 1	
			Capt. TURK & party of 8 Bearers, rejoined advanced dressing station party.	

1875 Wt. W593/826 1,000,000 4/15 J.B.C. & A. A.D.S.S./Forms/C. 2118.

Instructions regarding War Diaries and Intelligence Summaries are contained in F. S. Regs., Part II. and the Staff Manual respectively. Title Pages will be prepared in manuscript.

12

WAR DIARY
or
INTELLIGENCE SUMMARY
(Erase heading not required.)

Army Form C. 2118

Place 1915	Date	Hour	Summary of Events and Information	Remarks and references to Appendices
	July 31st		The Classification of wounded admitted during July is as in the accompanying chart APPENDIX I	
			Total admissions for July: Sick 574; Wounded 79; Gas asphyxiation 1; = 654. Total since Feb 3rd: Sick 5459; Wounded 5091; Gassed 575; = 11,125	
			The following Officers & NCOs of this unit were 'mentioned' in Sir John French's last Despatch. Lt. Col WHAIT. J.R; Major WAGGETT. E.B.; Capt. FAIRBANK. H.A.T; S/Sergt. BOYES. J.T. No. 66; S/Sergt. CASWELL. J.C. No. 679.	
			J. R. Whait Lt. Col. 85th (3rd London) Field Ambulance	

1875 Wt. W593/826 1,000,000 4/15 J.B.C. & A. A.D.S.S./Forms/C. 2118.

APPENDIX. I

CLASSIFICATION OF WOUNDED

ADMITTED TO 85TH FIELD AMBULANCE 1ST TO 31ST JULY (INCLUSIVE)

	Wounds of Head						Neck	Chest	Abdomen	Back			Arms						Legs							Total No DEATHS	Total No Wounds
	Scalp	Skull	Brain	Face	Jaw	Fract^d				Shoulders	Buttocks	Back	Humerus	Fract^d	Forearm	Fract^d	Hand	Fingers	Thigh	Fract^d	Knee	Lower Leg	Fract^d	Ankle	Foot		
Gunshot	2	3	-	3	-	1	-	4	2	6	3	-	-	1	1	1	-	1	1	-	-	-	-	-	2	·	31
									1																	1	
Shrapnel	2	4	-	-	-	-	-	2	-	2	4	3	-	-	3	1	1	-	2	-	1	3	2	-	2	-	32
		1																					1			2	
Grenade or Mortar	-	1	-	-	-	-	2	-	-	-	-	-	-	-	-	-	-	-	-	-	-	-	-	-	-	-	3
Accidental	-	-	-	-	-	-	-	-	-	-	-	-	-	-	-	-	4	4	-	-	-	-	-	-	5	-	13
	4	8		3		1	2	6	2	8	7	3		1	4	2	5	5	3		1	3	2		9		79

28th Division

121
6807

August 1915

85th Field Ambulance

Vol VIII

August 15.

ams

Army Form C. 2118

- Instructions regarding War Diaries and Intelligence Summaries are contained in F. S. Regs., Part II. and the Staff Manual respectively. Title Pages will be prepared in manuscript.

WAR DIARY
or
INTELLIGENCE SUMMARY
(Erase heading not required.)

Place	Date	Hour	Summary of Events and Information	Remarks and references to Appendices
1915	August 1st		Admitted Sick 7 Wounded 2 9 Transferred to Clearing H. 7 " " Convalt. Rest Camp 7 — Discharged to duty 6.	
	2nd		Admitted Sick 8 Wounded 2 10 Transferred to Clearing H. 2 " " Convalt. Rest Camp 1 — Discharged to duty 3	
			Turned out all the Bearers at 11 p.m. for a test mobilization. They were on parade ready to move off & equipped within 15 minutes of being called. Then marched them to Advanced Dressing Station 3¾ miles in 47 minutes. Return journey 55 minutes.	
			S/Sergt. CASWELL & 8 Bearers relieved advanced Dressing Station party	

1875 Wt. W593/826 1,000,000 4/15 J.B.C. & A. A.D.S.S./Forms/C. 2118.

2/

Army Form C. 2118

Instructions regarding War Diaries and Intelligence Summaries are contained in F. S. Regs., Part II. and the Staff Manual respectively. Title Pages will be prepared in manuscript.

WAR DIARY
or
INTELLIGENCE SUMMARY
(Erase heading not required.)

Place	Date	Hour	Summary of Events and Information	Remarks and references to Appendices
1915	August 3rd		admitted sick 10 including 2/Lieut HARTOPP. E.L. 1/Suffolks	
			wounded 6	
			16	
			Transferred to Clearing H. 6 discharged to duty 3.	
			" " Convalt Rest Camp 2	
	4th		admitted sick 9	
			wounded 3	
			12	
			Transferred to Clearing H. 2 discharged to duty 15	
			" " Convalt Rest Camp 5	
	5th		Sergt Marshall & 8 Bearers relieved advanced dressing station party.	
			Following men joined as reinforcement from ROUEN	
			No 2103 L/Corpl FRANCE. A.S.	
			" 29 Pte DUTTON W.A.	
			" 1205 " FOY. A.J	
			" 538 " MINTO. H	
			" 536 " ANDERSON. W	
			" 674 " HEBBORN. F.	
			" 690 " BUGDEN. W.J.	
			Lieut WOOTTON was detailed for temporary duty with the 5/K.O.R.L	

1875 Wt. W593/826 1,000,000 4/15 J.B.C. & A. A.D.S.S./Forms/C. 2118.

Army Form C. 2118.

Instructions regarding War Diaries and Intelligence Summaries are contained in F. S. Regs., Part II. and the Staff Manual respectively. Title Pages will be prepared in manuscript.

3

WAR DIARY
or
INTELLIGENCE SUMMARY
(Erase heading not required.)

Place	Date	Hour	Summary of Events and Information	Remarks and references to Appendices
1915	August 5th		Admitted Sick 11 including Capt. THACKRAY. J.N. 4 Suffolks, 2/Lieut. BENKE. L.L. Yorkshire Regt. attached 4/E. Yorks.	
			Wounded 5	
			16	
			= 8	
			Transferred to Clearing H. 8 Discharged to Duty 2.	
			" " Convalt. Rest Camp 4	
			Pte. PIERCE. H.C. 124 discharged to take up Commission in 3/3rd London Regiment.	
			Capt. H.A.T. FAIRBANK. applied to be transferred as Surgeon to a Base Hospl. I forwarded his application, reporting I could not recommend it, as primarily that all members of the unit volunteered for foreign service on condition they should only serve in this unit, & that if it was granted other Senior Officers would make similar applications in order to vary the monotony of service & interests of the unit would be seriously affected. A.D.M.S. supported this contention.	
			A number of cases of Albuminuria are now presenting themselves in this Division. So far cause is not ascertainable & they rapidly improve in hospital.	
			The majority of sick admitted are suffering from fever, up to 104°F, headache & pains in limbs. Temp. lasting 4 or 5 days & convalescence fairly slow in some cases, possibly Influenza. It has been suggested by Sir Wilmot Herringham as being due to an infection introduced by bites of flies. I have found no evidence of this yet.	

1875 Wt. W593/826 1,000,000 4/15 J.B.C. & A. A.D.S.S./Forms/C. 2118.

4

Army Form C. 2118

Instructions regarding War Diaries and Intelligence Summaries are contained in F. S. Regs., Part II. and the Staff Manual respectively. Title Pages will be prepared in manuscript.

WAR DIARY
or
INTELLIGENCE SUMMARY
(Erase heading not required.)

Place	Date	Hour	Summary of Events and Information	Remarks and references to Appendices
1915	Aug	6th	Admitted Sick 10 including Major TURNER F.C. Lord Strathconas Horse; Capt. FROST R.W. 14/Canadians; " COWPER W. 2/KORL; Lieut. DEIGHTON J. RAMC attd 5/KORL	
			Wounded 2 / 12	
			Transferred to Clearing H. 2	
			" " Convall. Rest Camp 7 — Discharged to duty 8	
		7th	Admitted Sick 10 including Lieut. HAWKINS A.E. R.F.A.; 2/Lieut. FRISBY L.C. 6/Welch	
			Wounded 3 / 13	
			Transferred to Clearing H. 2 — Discharged to duty 6	
			" " Convall. Rest Camp 0	
		8th	Admitted Sick 14 including Lieut. HODGKINSON A. 5/KORL; 2/Lieut. THOMPSTONE R. 3/S. Staffords attd 2/E. Surreys	
			Wounded 11 / 25	
			Transferred to Clearing H. 12 — Discharged to duty 4	
			" " Convall. Rest Camp 7	

1875 Wt. W593/826 1,000,000 4/15 J.B.C. & A. A.D.S.S./Forms/C. 2118.

5

Army Form C. 2118.

· Instructions regarding War Diaries and Intelligence Summaries are contained in F. S. Regs., Part II. and the Staff Manual respectively. Title Pages will be prepared in manuscript.

WAR DIARY
or
INTELLIGENCE SUMMARY
(Erase heading not required.)

Place	Date	Hour	Summary of Events and Information	Remarks and references to Appendices
1915	Aug	8th	Driver POULTON. L. No 032631. M.T. awarded 7 days Field Punishment No 1. for disobedience to Standing Orders, in leaving his Motor Ambulance unattended with engine running in BAILLEUL on 6th inst.	
			Corporal YATES. E. No 856. Reprimanded for being present & allowing Pte POULTON to commit the offence.	
		9th	admitted sick 19 wounded 2 21 Transferred to Clearing H. 6 " Conval. Rest Camp 5 Discharged to Duty 2.	
		10th	admitted sick 19 including Lieut D'ANTUN. A.A. Interpreter, attached 1/Welsh " BUTLER. H.A.R. 5/R.W. Surreys 2/Lieut. DEVEY. J.H.C. 3/Monmouths 2/ " WALLACE. ST. D. R.F.A. 2/ " YUNGE-BATEMAN. E.G. " wounded 2 21 Transferred to Clearing H. 4 " Conval. Rest Camp 9 Discharged to Duty 3 Died 1	

1875 Wt. W593/826 1,000,000 4/15 J.B.C. & A. A.D.S.S./Forms/C. 2118.

6

Army Form C. 2118

- Instructions regarding War Diaries and Intelligence Summaries are contained in F. S. Regs., Part II. and the Staff Manual respectively. Title Pages will be prepared in manuscript.

WAR DIARY
or
INTELLIGENCE SUMMARY

(Erase heading not required.)

Place	Date	Hour	Summary of Events and Information	Remarks and references to Appendices
1915	Aug	11th	Admitted Sick 12 including Lt/Col HUDSON. T.R.C. 17th Division, Ground Staff; Lieut. GWYTHER. G.M. 1/Suffolks; " LUCAS. A. Canadian Cavalry Brigade	
			Wounded 4 / 16	
			Transferred to Clearing H. 6	
			" " Convalt. Rest Camp 7 — Discharged to duty 5	
		12th	Admitted Sick 16 including Lieut. HEATH. J.W. 1/K.O.Y.L.I; " REDDAWAY. H. 3/Roy. Fus.; 2/Lieut. MARTINDALE. A.H. 1/K.O.Y.L.I; 2/ " GOODLIFFE. J.B. 8/Leicesters	
			Wounded 5 / 21	
			Transferred to Clearing H. 5	
			" " Convalt. Rest Camp 2 — Discharged to duty 10	
			Lieut. WOOTTON rejoined from temporary duty as M.O. with 5/K.O.R.L.	

1875 Wt. W593/826 1,000,000 4/15 J.B.C. & A. A.D.S.S./Forms/C. 2118.

· Instructions regarding War Diaries and Intelligence Summaries are contained in F. S. Regs., Part II. and the Staff Manual respectively. Title Pages will be prepared in manuscript.

7

WAR DIARY
or
INTELLIGENCE SUMMARY
(Erase heading not required.)

Army Form C. 2118

Place	Date	Hour	Summary of Events and Information	Remarks and references to Appendices
1915	Aug 12		following men advanced to 2nd Class Constables with 4th rate of Corps pay (6d) as from 11th inst. No. 175 L/Corpl. DEBENHAM. H.J.W. " 115 " PRATT C.H.D " 69 " WALTER. A.G.T. " 36 Pte. BALLARD. T " 296 " BRILL . C " 172 " DAVIS . G.H. " 126 " KENCHINGTON . F " 82 " POLLARD. P.G Our Tents which were coloured a Blackish brown, by means of Cutch 6 lbs to 2 gallons of water & Sulphate of Copper as a "Fixer" & boiled according to instructions of D.A.D.O.S ~~are~~ in order to diminish their visibility. [illegible] having then coloured & having become almost white again. [illegible] with 12 lbs Cutch to 2 gallons & boiled, leaving out the Copper Sulphate & painting the canvas while dry instead of wet (as previously instructed). The result is a light chestnut brown & several tents so done a fortnight ago show no signs of fading or colour being washed out by rain.	

1875 Wt. W593/826 1,000,000 4/15 J.B.C. & A. A.D.S.S./Forms/C. 2118.

Army Form C. 2118.

·Instructions regarding War Diaries and Intelligence Summaries are contained in F. S. Regs., Part II. and the Staff Manual respectively. Title Pages will be prepared in manuscript.

8

WAR DIARY
or
INTELLIGENCE SUMMARY
(Erase heading not required.)

Place	Date	Hour	Summary of Events and Information	Remarks and references to Appendices
1915	Aug	13th	Admitted Sick 10 Wounded 6 16	
			Transferred to Clearing H. 5 " " Convalt Rest Camp 10 Discharged to duty 5	
		14th	Captain Fairbank returned to Ambulance from duty with O.C. Section at Officers Convalescent Rest Station MONT NOIR.	
			S/Sergt CASWELL & 8 Bearers relieved party at advanced Dressing Station	
			Admitted Sick 8 including Major HOPE, J.W. D.A.Q.M.G. 28th Division " KNOX, G.S. R.E. " McGIBBON, G.D. 13th Batt. Canadians	
			Wounded 3 11	
			Transferred to Clearing H. 2 Discharged to duty 5 " " Convalt Rest Camp 5 including 2/Lieut HARTELL H.L. 3/Roy. F.	
		15th	Admitted Sick 13 Wounded 4 17	
			Transferred to Clearing H. 9 Discharged to duty 7 " " Convalt Rest Camp 2	

1875 Wt. W593/826 1,000,000 4/15 J.B.C. & A. A.D.S.S./Forms/C. 2118.

Army Form C. 2118

WAR DIARY
or
INTELLIGENCE SUMMARY
(Erase heading not required.)

Instructions regarding War Diaries and Intelligence Summaries are contained in F. S. Regs., Part II. and the Staff Manual respectively. Title Pages will be prepared in manuscript.

9

Place	Date	Hour	Summary of Events and Information	Remarks and references to Appendices
1915	Aug	16th	Admitted sick 20 including Major GRANT-THOROLD. R.S. 8/Roy. Fus.; Lieut. ALLEN. A.S. 8/ " "; Capt. LUCAS. R.H. RAMC attd. 8/ " "; " MONEY. H.G. 11/Middlesex	
			Wounded 5 / 25 [?]	
			Transferred to Clearing H. 3; " " Convalt. Rest Camp 2; Discharged to Duty 14.	
		17th	Sergt. Marshall + 8 Bearers rejoined party at advanced dressing station [?]	
			Admitted sick 13 including Major EVILL. C.A. 1/Monmouths; " LONG. C.E. 1/Canadian F. Artillery; Capt. McCARTHY. W.E.C. 1/ " [illegible]; " GOLDBERG. J.M. 6/Welsh	
			Wounded 4 / 17	
			Transferred to Convalt. Rest Camp 11; Transferred to Clearing H. [?] 7; Transferred to 53rd Field Amb. 4; Transferred to 2nd Canadian F. Amb. 2	
			Self inflicted wounds, Dental cases { Discharged to Duty 7; Died 1	
			All self inflicted wounds are to be transferred to a special Hospital run by the 53rd Field Ambulance at BOESCHEPPE, when Court of Enquiry + Court Martial will be held upon them	

Army Form C. 2118.

· Instructions regarding War Diaries and Intelligence Summaries are contained in F. S. Regs., Part II. and the Staff Manual respectively. Title Pages will be prepared in manuscript.

10

WAR DIARY
or
INTELLIGENCE SUMMARY
(Erase heading not required.)

Place	Date	Hour	Summary of Events and Information	Remarks and references to Appendices
	Aug	18th	Lieut. R.E. BARNSLEY proceeded to the Officers Convalescent Rest Station at MONTNOIR in relief of Lieut. ROBBINS who returned to Headquarters of the unit at WESTOUTRE.	
			Admitted Sick 10	
			Wounded 4	
			14	
			Transferred to Convalt. Rest Camp 10 — Discharged to duty 7	
			Transferred to Clearing H. 5	
		19th	MAJOR. WAGGETT. E.B. / S/Major. WALLER. F. / No 174 Pte WAREING. F. } will proceed on leave from 22nd to 26th inst.	
			Admitted (Sick 8 including Capt. ROBERTS. H. RFA 2nd Corps	
			Wounded 4	
			12	
			Transferred to Clearing H. 3 — Discharged to duty 4	
			" Convalt. Rest Camp 3	
			" 2 Canadian Field Amb 1 dental case.	
		20th	Sergt. Harris & 8 Bearers relieved party at Advanced Dressing Station	

Army Form C. 2118

WAR DIARY
or
INTELLIGENCE SUMMARY
(Erase heading not required.)

Instructions regarding War Diaries and Intelligence Summaries are contained in F. S. Regs., Part II. and the Staff Manual respectively. Title Pages will be prepared in manuscript.

11

Place	Date	Hour	Summary of Events and Information	Remarks and references to Appendices
	Aug	20th	Admitted Sick 13 including Major FISHER. D.L. 86th Field Ambulance RAMC	
			Lieut WARDLE. V. 86th " "	
			" WELLS. J 2/E. Yorks	
			" LEWIS. H.T. 6/Welsh	
			2/" POER. L.H. R.F.A.	
			Wounded 2	
			15	
			Transferred to Clearing H. 4	
			" " Convalt Rest Camp 5 — Discharged to duty 1.	
			" " 2nd Canadian Field Amb 1 mental case	
		21st	Lieut WOOTTON was detailed for duty as M.O. i/c 1/K.O.Y.L.I till Sept 6th	
			No 42 Pte ROBINSON. L.W. awarded 28 days Field Punishment No 1. for being found asleep at his post as sentry at MONT NOIR between 6 & 7 am 19th	
			No 189 Pte SUTTON. A.G. joined from No 8 Sanitary Section 6th Division	
			Admitted Sick 16. including Capt LINDSAY. S.B. 13/Canadian Batt.	
			" BARNARD. W.G.F. 2/Buffs	
			Lieut McCLURE. K.H. 1/NORTHANTS attd No 9 Entrenching Batt.	
			Wounded 3	
			19	
			Transferred to Clearing H. 6	
			" Convalt Rest Camp 6 Self inflicted wound	
			" 53rd Field Amb 1	
			" 2nd Canadian Field Amb 1 mental case — Discharged to duty 3.	

1875 Wt. W593/826 1,000,000 4/15 J.B.C. & A. A.D.S.S./Forms/C. 2118.

Army Form C. 2118.

*Instructions regarding War Diaries and Intelligence Summaries are contained in F. S. Regs., Part II. and the Staff Manual respectively. Title Pages will be prepared in manuscript.

12

WAR DIARY
or
INTELLIGENCE SUMMARY

(Erase heading not required.)

Place	Date	Hour	Summary of Events and Information	Remarks and references to Appendices
	Aug	22nd	Admitted Sick 9 including Capt. BUXTON. V. 3/Leinster attd 2/5 Norths " HILL. A.R 3/Cheshires 2/Lieut ADDENBROOKE PROUT. R R.G.A. & R.F.C. Wounded 2 11 Transferred to Clearing H. 4 Discharged to duty 9 " " Convalt Rest Camp 4	
		23rd.	No. 189. Pte SUTTON. A.G. transferred to 84th Field ambulance The LADY WANTAGE Soup Kitchen which has been attached to this unit for several months, proceeded with Driver WILLETTS (British Red Cross Soc) to BOULOGNE for overhaul. Started Route marches for the Bearers on alternate days during the quiet period. Admitted Sick 7 including 2/Lieut WELCH. L.A 1/KOYLI Wounded 3 10 Transferred to Clearing H. 3 " " Convalt Rest Camp 4 " 62nd Canadian Field amb 2 dental cases. Discharged to Duty 2 Died 1	

Instructions regarding War Diaries and Intelligence Summaries are contained in F. S. Regs., Part II. and the Staff Manual respectively. Title Pages will be prepared in manuscript.

13

Army Form C. 2118.

WAR DIARY
or
INTELLIGENCE SUMMARY
(Erase heading not required.)

Place	Date	Hour	Summary of Events and Information	Remarks and references to Appendices
	Aug	24th	Band of the 83rd Brigade played in our Hospital Camp from 5 till 7 p.m.	
			Admitted Sick 8 including Capt. MILNER. G.C. 5/K.O.R.L.	
			Wounded 8 / 16	
			Transferred to Clearing St. 10 — Discharged to duty 5	
			" Convalt. Rest Camp 6	
		25th	Admitted Sick 10 including Revd. Capt. ROYSE. T.H. C.F. 83rd Brigade; 2/Lieut. TERRELL. A.C. 3/Middlesex	
			Wounded 2 / 12	
			Transferred to Clearing St. 1 — Discharged to duty 3	
			Convalt. Rest Camp 1	
		26th	Sergt. OUSTON & 8 Bearers relieved Advanced Dressing Station party	
			Admitted Sick 9 including Capt. DEED. W.R.W. 5/K.O. ~~2nd~~ R.L.; Lieut. SECCOMBE. H.C. 10/Canadian Batt.; " JONES. H.C. 3/Toronto Batt.; 2/" MORRIS. H. 3/Middlesex; 2/" MACLEOD-WASSE. F. R.G.A.	
			Wounded 13 / 22	
			Transferred to Clearing St. 4 — Discharged to duty 5	
			" " Convalt. Rest Camp 5	

1875 Wt. W593/826 1,000,000 4/15 J.B.C. & A. A.D.S.S./Forms/C. 2118.

Army Form C. 2118

Instructions regarding War Diaries and Intelligence Summaries are contained in F. S. Regs., Part. II. and the Staff Manual respectively. Title Pages will be prepared in manuscript.

14

WAR DIARY
or
INTELLIGENCE SUMMARY
(Erase heading not required.)

Imp. Hav., 26/7 — 10.000

Place	Date	Hour	Summary of Events and Information	Remarks and references to Appendices
	Aug	27th	Admitted Sick 16 including Lt-Col ROBERTS, A.C. 3/Roy. Fusiliers	
			Wounded 1 / 17	
			Transferred to Clearing H. 4	
			" " Convalt: Rest Camp 5 Discharged to duty 2.	
		28th	Sergt-Major WALLER, F. + Pte WARING F. reported for duty off leave	
			Admitted Sick 16 including 2/Lieut CAMERON, T.S. 2/Cheshires	
			Wounded 2 / 18	
			Transferred to Clearing H. 8	
			Convalt Rest Camp 4 Discharged to duty 4	
			" " 2nd Canadian F. Amb 3 Dental Cases	
		29th	S/Sergt BOYES + 8 Bearers relieved [illegible] Station Party	
			Lieut SMITH R.V. detailed for duty as M.O. i/c 5/R.O.R.L until Sept 7th	

Army Form C. 2118.

Instructions regarding War Diaries and Intelligence Summaries are contained in F. S. Regs., Part. II. and the Staff Manual respectively. Title Pages will be prepared in manuscript.

15

WAR DIARY
or
INTELLIGENCE SUMMARY
(Erase heading not required.)

Imp. Hav., 26/7 — 10.000

Place	Date	Hour	Summary of Events and Information	Remarks and references to Appendices
	Aug	29th	Admitted sick 14. including Capt CAZALET. G.L. 9/Roy Fusiliers	
			" ANNESLEY. F.C. 8/ " "	
			2/Lieut CARTLEDGE. C.H. 5/ Northumberland F.	
			Wounded 2 / 16	
			Transferred to Clearing H. 3	
			" " Conval. Rest Camp 8 Discharged to duty 3	
		30th	Major WAGGETT. E.B. reported for duty off leave.	
			Admitted sick 15 including Capt FULLER. C.S. 7/E Surrey	
			Wounded 4 / 19	
			Transferred to Clearing H. 5 Discharged to duty 3	
			" " 2nd Canadian [illegible] 1 [illegible]	

Instructions regarding War Diaries and Intelligence Summaries are contained in F. S. Regs., Part. II. and the Staff Manual respectively. Title Pages will be prepared in manuscript.

16

WAR DIARY
or
INTELLIGENCE SUMMARY

(Erase heading not required.)

Army Form C. 2118.

Imp. Hav., 26/7 — 10,000

Place	Date	Hour	Summary of Events and Information	Remarks and references to Appendices
1915	Aug	31st	Admitted Sick 11 including Major FULCHER. W 3/Middlesex Capt. BOND. C.M. 1/KOYLI 2/Lieut. TOLLER. RA. 1/Welsh 2/ " DARBY. W.E. 1/Monmouths Wounded 9 20 Transferred to Clearing H. 6 " " Convalt. Rest Camp 5 Discharged to Duty 1, Died 1 Arranged for all Officers on Convoy duty & evacuating Regt. aid Post to always carry a Esmarch's Rubber tourniquet with them, in consequence of several cases having occurred in which patients have died of haemorrhage as the result of the regulation tourniquet or improvised tourniquets applied in the trenches to have either slipped or being insufficiently applied. Since then a concert party formed by our men have frequently given Concerts to the Brigade while in billets, which have been a great success.	

Army Form C. 2118

17

Instructions regarding War Diaries and Intelligence Summaries are contained in F. S. Regs., Part. II. and the Staff Manual respectively. Title Pages will be prepared in manuscript.

WAR DIARY
or
INTELLIGENCE SUMMARY
(Erase heading not required.)

Imp. Hav., 26/7 — 10.000

Place	Date	Hour	Summary of Events and Information	Remarks and references to Appendices
1915	Aug	31st	The classification of wounded admitted during August is shown in the accompanying Chart APPENDIX I	
			Total admissions for August: Sick 371, Wounded 128 — 499	
			Total since Feb 3rd: Sick 5830, Wounded 5219, Gassed 575 — 11.624	

[signature] Lt. Col.
O.C. 1/5th (3rd London) Field Ambulance
23rd Division

APPENDIX. I

CLASSIFICATION OF WOUNDED

ADMITTED TO 85TH (3RD LON. T.) FIELD AMBULANCE – 1ST TO 31ST AUGUST 1915 (INCLUSIVE)

	WOUNDS OF HEAD						NECK	CHEST	ABDOMEN	BACK.			ARMS.						LEGS.							TOTAL Nº DEATHS	TOTAL Nº WOUNDS.
	SCALP	SKULL	BRAIN	FACE	JAW.	FRACT.				SHOULDERS	BUTTOCK	BACK.	HUMERUS	FRACT.D	FOREARM.	FRACT.D	HAND	FINGERS	THIGH.	FRACT.	KNEE	L'R. LEG	FRACT.	ANKLE	FOOT		
GUNSHOT.	5	6	1	6		1	1	3 1	1 1	2	1 1	3	2		7	3	6	4	4 1	1	2	3			3	4	65
SHRAPNEL.	5	4		4				1		1		3			4		3		7		1	1		1	1		36
GRENADE OR MORTAR.	2		1	4				1			4				1			1	2		1						17
ACCIDENTAL				1								1			1			2							1		6
	12	10	2	15		1	1	6	2	3	6	7	2		13	3	9	7	14	1	4	4		1	5		124

[illegible signature]

CLASSIFICATION OF WOUNDED.

28th Division

121/7051

Sept 1915

85th Field Ambulance

Vol IX

Sept 15

Instructions regarding War Diaries and Intelligence Summaries are contained in F. S. Regs., Part. II. and the Staff Manual respectively. Title Pages will be prepared in manuscript.

WAR DIARY
or
INTELLIGENCE SUMMARY

(Erase heading not required.)

Army Form C. 2118

Imp. Hav., 26/7 — 10.000

Place	Date	Hour	Summary of Events and Information	Remarks and references to Appendices
1915				
Sept	1st		Admitted Sick 12 including Capt: ALLAN.O.H.? / North'd Fusiliers 2/Lieut. MOORE.E.A. 11/Middlesex Lieut. ARMOUR.E.B.A. Canadian F. A.	
			Wounded 4 16	
			Transferred to Clearing H. 6 — Discharged to duty 8 " Conval Rest Camp 7 — " duty with No 15 Sanitary Sect. 2 10	
			Sergt: WARD + 8 Bearers relieved the party at advanced Dressing Station.	
	2nd		Admitted Sick 10 including Capt: RICHARDS.J.S. 6/Welch	
			Wounded 3 13	
			Transferred to Clearing H. 2 " Conval: Rest Camp 3 " No 24 Stationary Hosp. ARQUES 2 — (Eye cases). Discharged to duty 13	
	3rd		Admitted Sick 3 Wounded 4 7	
			Transferred to Clearing H. 3 — Discharged to duty 1 " Conval: Rest Camp 5 — Died 1	

Army Form C. 2118

Instructions regarding War Diaries and Intelligence Summaries are contained in F. S. Regs., Part. II. and the Staff Manual respectively. Title Pages will be prepared in manuscript.

2

WAR DIARY
or
INTELLIGENCE SUMMARY
(Erase heading not required.)

Imp. Hav., 26/7 — 10.000

Place 1915	Date	Hour	Summary of Events and Information	Remarks and references to Appendices
Sept.	4th		Admitted sick 7 including Capt. EKINS. J.M. 2/Canadian artillery	
			wounded 1	
			8	
			Transferred to Clearing H. 2	
			" Convalt. Rest Camp 4 — Discharged to duty 1	
			Lt Col J R. WHAIT. proceeded on 7 days leave to England	
	5th		Admitted sick 9 including Capt. MIRRILEES. F.D. [illegible]	
			wounded 8	
			17	
			Transferred to Clearing H. 6	
			" Convalt. Rest Camp 5 — Discharged to duty 10	
			" 53rd Field Amb. 1 – (self inflicted wound)	
			No. 84 Pte CHRISTOPHERSON. D. reported to O.C. 28th Batt. LONDON REGT. G.H.Q. preparatory to undergoing course of instruction for a commission at Cadet School ST OMER. (authority A.G. G.H.Q. 9/1158/264/d. 2.9.15)	
	6th		Admitted sick 15 including 2/Lieut BENHAM. M.E. 3/Middlesex, 2/ " AMBROSE. G.E. R.E	
			wounded 2	
			17	
			Transferred to Clearing H. 5	
			" Convalt. Rest Camp 2	
			" Canadian Field Amb. 2 – (dental cases)	

3

Instructions regarding War Diaries and Intelligence Summaries are contained in F. S. Regs., Part. II. and the Staff Manual respectively. Title Pages will be prepared in manuscript.

WAR DIARY
or
INTELLIGENCE SUMMARY
(Erase heading not required.)

Army Form C. 2118

Imp. Hav., 26/7 — 10.000

Place 1915	Date	Hour	Summary of Events and Information	Remarks and references to Appendices
Sept:	6th		No. 216 Pte. CUTCLIFFE. J. selected to report to O.C. 28th Batt: LONDON Regt. G.H.Q. preparatory to undergoing a course of instruction for a Commission at Cadet School	
			Lieut. SMITH. K.V. reported for duty on completion of duty with 5/K.O.R.L.	
	7th		Admitted sick 6 including 2/Lieut. HENSON. J. 2/K.O.R.L. Capt: PEAKE. M.C. 2/ " wounded 4 10	
			Transferred to Clearing Stn. 3 " " Convalt: Rest Camp 4 " " Canadian Field Amb. 1 – (dental case)	
			Corpl. Cross & 8 Bearers relieved party at Advanced Dressing Station	
			Lieut. WOOTTON reported for duty on completion of duty with 1/K.O.Y.L.I.	
	8th		Admitted sick 9 including 2/Lieut. WEST. G. 1/Suffolks wounded 4 13	
			Transferred to Clearing Stn. 10 . Discharged to duty 2 " Convalt: Rest Camp 3	

Army Form C. 2118

4 Instructions regarding War Diaries and Intelligence Summaries are contained in F. S. Regs., Part II. and the Staff Manual respectively. Title Pages will be prepared in manuscript.

WAR DIARY
or
INTELLIGENCE SUMMARY
(Erase heading not required.)

Imp. Hav., 26/7 — 40,000

Place	Date	Hour	Summary of Events and Information	Remarks and references to Appendices
1915 Sept.	9th		Admitted Sick 16 including Capt. MOSS-BLUNDELL S.W. 1/KOYLI, 2/Lieut. FRIEND. B. 6/Roy W. Kents.	
			Wounded 8 / 24	
			Transferred to Clearing H. 10	
			" " Conval. Rest Camp 3	
			QMS. CANHAM. H.W.H. No. 74 & Corpl. WILLETT. J. proceeded on 5 days leave to England.	
			S/Major WALLER. F. reported sick with acute nephritis.	
	10th		Admitted Sick 10 including Lieut. HARROLD. W 5/KORL	
			Wounded 3 / 13	
			Transferred to Clearing H. 6	
			" " Conval. Rest Camp 3	
			" " Canadian Field Amb. 1 – (dental case) Discharged to duty 5.	
			Sergt. RUSSELL proceeded on 1 month's leave to England upon signing on for continuation & duration of war.	
	11th		Admitted Sick 13 including Capt. DYAS. V.W. 4/Canadian Batt., Lieut. LYNN. E.W. Canadian R.E., " LEWIS. H.E. 6/Welsh	
			Wounded 6 / 19	
			Transferred to Clearing H. 6	
			" " Conval. Rest Camp 2	
			" " Canadian Field Amb. 1 – (dental case)	
			Discharged to duty 5	

5.

Instructions regarding War Diaries and Intelligence Summaries are contained in F. S. Regs., Part II. and the Staff Manual respectively. Title Pages will be prepared in manuscript.

WAR DIARY
or
INTELLIGENCE SUMMARY
(Erase heading not required.)

Army Form C. 2118

Imp. Hav., 26/7 — 10,000

Place 1915	Date	Hour	Summary of Events and Information	Remarks and references to Appendices
Sept.	11th		Tube Helmets issued to unit. & men instructed in use of same.	
			Driver KENDAL. (MT. ASC) awarded 14 days F.P. No 2 for refusal to obey orders of N.C.O. i/c Parade.	
	12th		Admitted sick 7	
			wounded 3	
			10	
			Transferred to Clearing H. 7	
			" " Conval. Rest Camp 8	
			" " 53rd Field Amb 1 – (self inflicted wound) Discharged to Duty 5.	
	13th		Admitted sick 20	
			wounded 3	
			23	
			Transferred to Clearing H 5 Discharged to duty 3.	
			" " Conval. Rest Camp 5	
			Sergt HARRIE & 8 Bearers relieved party at Advanced Dressing Station	
			No M/2 032638 a/Sergt. FEA. A.B. promoted to permanent rank of Sergeant from June 1st 15	
			" M/2 022294 2/Corp. WILLETTS. J. " " a/Corpl " from March 1st 15	
			" M/2 032629 Pte DACK. H " " a/Corpl " " 1st 15	
			Lt. Col. [illegible] WHAIT. returned to duty off leave.	

Army Form C. 2118

Instructions regarding War Diaries and Intelligence Summaries are contained in F. S. Regs., Part II. and the Staff Manual respectively. Title Pages will be prepared in manuscript.

6

WAR DIARY
or
INTELLIGENCE SUMMARY
(Erase heading not required.)

Imp. Hav., 26/7 — 10 000

Place 1915	Date	Hour	Summary of Events and Information	Remarks and references to Appendices
Sept.	14th		Admitted Sick 11 including Capt: JONES. P.B. 3/Middlesex " McCOMB. H.A. 4/Canadian Batt. Lieut. ROY. R. 14/ " " " BURBIDGE G.C. 10/ " " Wounded 0 11	
			Transferred to Clearing H. 8 " " Convalt. Rest Camp 3 " " Canadian Field amb 1 – (mental case) Discharged to duty 6.	
			Interpreter R. LABRE awarded 8 days confinement to his room by Officer of Liaison 28th Division for breach of discipline. (Striking another interpreter of superior rank in a quarrel).	
			Appointment: Col: N.C. FERGUSON. C.M.G. appointed from A.D.M.S 28th Div. to D.D.M.S 12th Army Corps. is succeeded by Col. N TYACKE.	
			All wheeled transport vehicles overhauled & repainted.	
	15th		Admitted Sick 8 Wounded 5 13	
			Transferred to Clearing H 10 " " Convalt. Rest Camp 4 " " Canadian Field amb 1 – (mental case) Discharged to duty 4	
			Collected 2000 Bricks from Brick Yard PONT DE NIEPPE for purpose of bricking horse lines.	

Army Form C. 2118

Instructions regarding War Diaries and Intelligence Summaries are contained in F. S. Regs., Part II. and the Staff Manual respectively. Title Pages will be prepared in manuscript.

7

WAR DIARY
or
INTELLIGENCE SUMMARY

(Erase heading not required.)

Imp. Hav., 26/7 — 10,000

Place	Date	Hour	Summary of Events and Information	Remarks and references to Appendices
1915 Sept.	15th		Sergt. UNDERHILL. F. proceeded on 1 month's leave to England on re-engaging for duration of war.	
			B. Section took over the new Convent at WESTOUTRE in which to open up Hospital for medical cases, removed from the Camp Hospital – by order of G.O.C.	
	16th		Admitted Sick 15 including 2/Lieut. GREW. B.D. 2/Northumbd Fusiliers, 2/ " BACON. D.F.C. 4/ D.L.I. attached 2/Northd Fus.	
			Wounded 1 / 16	
			Transferred to Clearing H. 3	
			" " Convalt. Rest Camp 3 / 3 Discharged to duty 3.	
			Corpl. TURK & 8 Bearers relieved party at advanced Dressing Station	
			Following were advanced to 4th rate of Corps pay as from March 9th 15 & further advanced to 3rd rate of Corps pay as from 8th Sept. 1915	
			No. 175 L/Corp. DEBENHAM. H.J.N.	
			" 116 " PRATT. C.H.D	
			" 69 " WALTER. A.G.T.	
			" 36 Pte. BALLARD. T.	
			" " BRILL. C	
			" 296 " DAVIES. G.H.	
			" 172 " KENCHINGTON. F.	
			" 126 "	
			" 82 " POLLARD. P.G.	

8

Army Form C. 2118

Instructions regarding War Diaries and Intelligence Summaries are contained in F. S. Regs., Part II. and the Staff Manual respectively. Title Pages will be prepared in manuscript.

WAR DIARY
or
INTELLIGENCE SUMMARY
(Erase heading not required.)

Imp. Hay., 26/7 – 10.000

Place	Date	Hour	Summary of Events and Information	Remarks and references to Appendices
1915				
Sept.	16th		The following were advanced to 4th rate of Corps pay as from 8th inst.	
			No 202 L/Corpl STEVENS. H.F.	
			" 347 Pte BAYNES. F.A.	
			" 162 " CURTIS. A.J.	
			" 139 " EILOART. C.H.	
			" 136 " GEARING. S.	
			" 142 " IZOD. F.	
			" 120 " KRANINGER. G.	
			" 267 " ROSE. E.A.	
	17th		Admitted Sick 9. including Lieut. POWER J. 2/Canadian Batt.	
			" STRATHEY. J.H.G. 2/ " "	
			" CHEVALIER. P. 3/ " "	[illegible]
			Wounded 1 / 10	
			Transferred to Clearing H.P. 3 — Discharged to duty 10.	
			" " Convalt. Rest Camp 1	
	18th		Admitted Sick 11 including Lieut. FRANKLIN. H.V. 7/Norfolks	
			Wounded 5 / 16	
			Transferred to Clearing H. 5 — Discharged to duty 5.	
			" " Convalt. Rest Camp 2	

9

Instructions regarding War Diaries and Intelligence Summaries are contained in F. S. Regs., Part II. and the Staff Manual respectively. Title Pages will be prepared in manuscript.

WAR DIARY
or
INTELLIGENCE SUMMARY
(Erase heading not required.)

Army Form C. 2118

Imp. Hav., 26/7 — 10.000

Place	Date	Hour	Summary of Events and Information	Remarks and references to Appendices
1915				
Sept.	18th		Captain FAIRBANK. H.A.T. proceeded on 7 days leave to England & following on 5 days leave.	
			Sergt. HARRIE. S.M.	
			Pte. SMITH. H	
			" HUGHES. T.C.	
			" OWEN. H.B.P.	
			Drvr. PARKER. W.J.	
	19th		Admitted Sick 7, wounded 3 — 10	
			Transferred to Clearing H. 7 — Discharged to duty 9.	
			" " Cornwall Rest Camp 2	
			Changed all iron rations which have been issued over 6 months.	
			Corpl. DILLON & 8 Bearers relieved party at Advanced Dressing Station	
			L/Corpl. STEVENS H.F. appointed Chiropodist in the unit, with additional pay at 2d per day.	
	20th		Admitted Sick 11, wounded 1 — 12 — Discharged to duty 17.	
			Transferred to Clearing H. 1	
			" " Cornwall Rest Camp 7	
			" " 4th Canadian Field Amb. 26 — on taking over from this unit — including 12 Officers at MONT. NOIR.	

10

Instructions regarding War Diaries and Intelligence Summaries are contained in F. S. Regs., Part II. and the Staff Manual respectively. Title Pages will be prepared in manuscript.

WAR DIARY
or
INTELLIGENCE SUMMARY
(Erase heading not required.)

Army Form C. 2118

Imp. Hav., 26/7 — 40,000

Place 1915	Date	Hour	Summary of Events and Information	Remarks and references to Appendices
Sept.	20th		a/Corpl. WILLETTS J. No. M/2.022294 } promoted to Corporal to date a/Corpl. DACK H. " M/2.032629 } from June 1st 1915 The unit ordered to move with 84th Brigade to PRADELLE on 21st inst. Packed equipment & handed over Hospital & Billets at WESTOUTRE to 4th Canadian Field Ambulance, 2nd Canadian Division. [illegible] Sent all surplus equipment to the HOSPICE. LOCRE.	
	21st		Lieut. ROBBINS with 2 Horse ambulances rendezvoused with 84th Brigade at 9 am & followed in rear of Brigade to pick up stragglers until the march. = 1/Welsh 6/Welsh 1/Suffolks 2/Cheshires 2/Northumberland Fus. Main body of unit rendezvoused at LOCRE at 1 pm & marched with Baggage & Supply Column of Brigade via BAILLEUL – STRAZEELE to PRADELLE – arrived 4.30 pm & established Hospital at School & billeted personnel in field adjoining the Chateau. Rations for 300 patients. 7 Motor Ambulances laden with 56 Stretchers & 12 Bell Tents reported to O/c Mechanical Workshop 28th Division provided with that unit – Drivers with 3 days rations.	

11

Instructions regarding War Diaries and Intelligence Summaries are contained in F. S. Regs., Part II. and the Staff Manual respectively. Title Pages will be prepared in manuscript.

WAR DIARY
or
INTELLIGENCE SUMMARY
(Erase heading not required.)

Army Form C. 2118

Imp. Hav., 26/7 — 10,000

Place 1915	Date	Hour	Summary of Events and Information	Remarks and references to Appendices
Sept	21st		On arrival despatched a motor cyclist to inform A.D.M.S of my location & to keep up communication.	
			"C" Section opened up under Capt VICK.	
			Admitted Sick 2	
	22nd		No 856 Corpl. YATES. E proceeded on 1 months leave to England on re-engaging for duration of the war.	
			Collected sick from billets of the Brigade	
			Admitted sick 15	
			Transferred to Clearing H. 4	
	23rd		Route marched the men	
			No 87 Driver WATT. W.R. left to report to 28th Batt LONDON, REGT to undergo 14 days Training prior to attending course at G.H.Q. Cadet School St OMER for Commission	
			Q.M.S. CANHAM appointed acting Sergt. major.	
			Admitted Sick 18	
			Transferred to ~~Duty~~ Clearing H 1 discharged to Duty 10	

12

Army Form C. 2118

Instructions regarding War Diaries and Intelligence Summaries are contained in F. S. Regs., Part II. and the Staff Manual respectively. Title Pages will be prepared in manuscript.

WAR DIARY
or
INTELLIGENCE SUMMARY

(Erase heading not required.)

Imp. Hav., 26/7 – 10,000

Place 1915	Date	Hour	Summary of Events and Information	Remarks and references to Appendices
Sept.	24th		'B' Section opened up a Hospital in boys School BORRE.	
			Capt. TURK & 6 men detailed to supervise filling of all Regimental water carts at HAZEBROUCK & see that the water in each is chlorinated before carts leave.	
			Lieut. WOOTTON detailed to act as M.O. to 130th Howitzer Brigade RFA temporarily.	
			Driver DOBSON.W.T. & Pte DUCKETT. J.E. proceeded on 5 days leave to England.	
			Orders to keep 1 Section in readiness to move at half an hours notice, & remainder of the unit in 1 hour.	
			C Section packed its equipment accordingly. A Section opening up for hospital duty at PRADELLE.	
			Admitted Sick 16	
			Transferred to Clearing H. 7	
	25th		Admitted Sick 19 including Capt. ROXBY. F.F. 1/Suffolks, 2/Lieut. HARTOPP. E.L 1/ " , 2/ " WRIGHT 1/ "	
			Transferred to Clearing H. 5	
			" " Conval. Rest Station MONT DES CATS 4	
			Discharged to duty 6.	

13

Instructions regarding War Diaries and Intelligence Summaries are contained in F. S. Regs., Part II. and the Staff Manual respectively. Title Pages will be prepared in manuscript.

WAR DIARY
or
INTELLIGENCE SUMMARY
(Erase heading not required.)

Army Form C. 2118

Imp. Hav., 26/7 — 10,000

Place	Date	Hour	Summary of Events and Information	Remarks and references to Appendices
1915 Sept.	25th		Orders from 84th Brigade H.Q. to move forward with Brigade at 7-30 am. 26th	
	26th		Admitted Sick 20	
			Transferred to Clearing H. 50 Discharged to duty 3.	
			All sick evacuated by 3 am. Unit packed up + marched at 8. am from Billets. to Starting point of Column PETIT SEC BOIS 9.1 am thence to MERVILLE.	
			Capt. POTTER + the Interpreter met Staff Capt. at 7-15 + proceeded on billeting duty.	
			Brigade + unit markings removed from vehicles in all division.	
			Continued march to Billet in field just N. of PARADIS.	
			Admitted + Transferred Sick 8	
	27th			
	27th	10 am	84th Brigade proceeded by Motor Busses to BETHUNE – thence by march route via BEUVRY to NOYELLES.	
			Tent division of the Field Ambulance accompanied Bearer Division in Busses. + 3 Motor Ambulances loaded with equipment to establish a Dressing Station. 1 Officer + 16 Bearers with Stretchers to Transport. Baggage guard + remainder of Ambulances proceeded with 1st Line Transport.	

Instructions regarding War Diaries and Intelligence Summaries are contained in F. S. Regs., Part II. and the Staff Manual respectively. Title Pages will be prepared in manuscript.

14

WAR DIARY
or
INTELLIGENCE SUMMARY
(Erase heading not required.)

Army Form C. 2118

Imp. Hav., 26/7 — 10,000

Place 1915	Date	Hour	Summary of Events and Information	Remarks and references to Appendices
Sept	27th		Bivouaced for the night at NOYELLES.	
	28th	8 am	Detailed Lieut ROBBINS 4 NCOs & 20 Bearers to proceed in motor ambulances to VERMELLES to learn the route & see the advanced dressing Stations to be taken over from the 29th Field Ambulance. Lieut Robbins reported to me at 1 pm that he had conducted the party under a guide from the 29th F. Amb. to the 2 advanced Dr. Stations & along the medical trench as far as our support trench. On his return as the trench (medical communication) was being shelled with H.E. he left 8 men in the BARTS dugouts & took the other 12 back to the Brewery (one of the Ad: D. Stations). Later 4 of the 8 returned to him at the other Advanced D. Station. He returned with the 16 men & 2 motor ambulances, & 4 remained in the dug outs. Shortly afterwards Pte SPOONER returned & informed me that his squad of 4 men had been ordered by the M.O. of 29th Field Amb at the dugouts to go up to the captured German trench & bring in some of the wounded lying there. They had not proceeded 200 yards when they were hit by a H.E. shell & No 345 Pte GOODYEAR. R.C & No 134 Pte KRANINGER. G. were killed & No 265 Pte LION. T.E. was wounded. Pte SPOONER F.P. was unhurt.	

Instructions regarding War Diaries and Intelligence Summaries are contained in F. S. Regs., Part II. and the Staff Manual respectively. Title Pages will be prepared in manuscript.

15

WAR DIARY
or
INTELLIGENCE SUMMARY
(Erase heading not required.)

Army Form C. 2118

Imp. Hav., 26/7 — 10,000

Place 1915	Date	Hour	Summary of Events and Information	Remarks and references to Appendices
Sept.	28th	2 pm	Lieut. ROBBINS, Lieut. BARNSLEY, Lieut. TAYLOR, Lieut. SMITH } & the Bearer Division with Equipment to fix up 2 advanced dressing Stations proceeded to VERMELLES & took over the Brewery & the BARTS Dugouts from the [illegible] Field Ambulance	
		3 pm	I took over the dressing Station at the SCHOOL at SAILLY-LABOURSE. B & C Sections Tent subdivisions opened up at School & Capt. POTTER with Tent subdivision of A Section took over the dressing Station for lightly wounded from [illegible] Field Amb.	
		4 pm	I proceeded to VERMELLES & went over the advanced dressing Station & medical communicating Trench, & arranged how the work there should be organised.	
		8 pm	Everything running smoothly. The Roof of cellar at the Brewery is being shored up by R.E. as it was threatening to fall in.	
			Admitted Sick 23, wounded 123 = 148 including Lieut. BOON G.E. 2/E. Kent; 2/Lt. SELBY M. 2/E. "; Lieut. CAMERON M. 12/Roy Scots; " GILLETT E.F. R.F.A.	
			Transferred to Clearing Station 143	

Army Form C. 2118

Instructions regarding War Diaries and Intelligence Summaries are contained in F. S. Regs., Part II. and the Staff Manual respectively. Title Pages will be prepared in manuscript.

16

WAR DIARY
or
INTELLIGENCE SUMMARY
(Erase heading not required.)

Imp. Hav., 26/7 — 10,000

Place	Date	Hour	Summary of Events and Information	Remarks and references to Appendices
1915				
Sept	29th		No. 72. L/Corpl. SMITH. E. F. rejoined the unit. (wounded at YPRES).	
			No. 127. Pte HUMPHREYS. D. wounded at VERMELLES. dressing Station evacuated.	
			Admitted Sick 62	
			Wounded 338 including Capt. BUCKLEY. E. 1/York & Lancs	
			400 — 2/Lieut. ADSETTS. W. H. 1/ " "	
			2/ " FLEMING-SANDS A. J. 2/E. Surrey	
			2/ " WILLIAMS. W. T. 2/E. KENTS	
			Lieut. MAINTLE. H. 2/E. "	
			" WHYTE. E. M. 3/Roy Fusiliers	
			CLARK. A. J. R. 3/ " "	
			2/Lieut. BISSELL. J 3/ " "	
			Transferred to Clearing H. 400	
			Discharged to duty 2	
			Died 2	
	30th		No. 295 Pte RAYSON. T. G. joined from Reserve unit as reinforcement.	
			Admitted Sick 29	
			Wounded 133 including Capt. ROW. G. W. 3/Middlesex	
			162 — 2/Lieut TERRELL. A. C. 3/ "	
			2/ " HOLLIS. J. N. 1/York & Lancs	
			2/ " HARTILL. H. L. 3/Roy. Fusiliers	
			Capt. SYKES. C. H. 3/ "	
			Transferred to Clearing H. 159 — Major BROWNE. F. M. R.E. 38/Field Co	
			Discharged to Duty 3 — " MONRO. J. D. R.E. 90/ " "	
			Died 1	

17

Instructions regarding War Diaries and Intelligence Summaries are contained in F. S. Regs., Part II. and the Staff Manual respectively. Title Pages will be prepared in manuscript.

WAR DIARY
or
INTELLIGENCE SUMMARY
(Erase heading not required.)

Army Form C. 2118

Imp. Hav., 26/7 — 10.000

Place 1915	Date	Hour	Summary of Events and Information	Remarks and references to Appendices
Sept	25th		The System of evacuation of wounded from in front of VERMELLE & which works well is: (1) 90 Bearers & 3 Officers are established at the advanced Dressing Station in the cellars of the ruined Brewery where necessary dressings are done (2) 30 Bearers & 1 Officer are at the 'Bart's' Dugout in the Medical Communicating Trench where wounded are temporarily collected & urgent dressings done — from these 30 men, 1 squad is detailed to remain at HAYWARDS HEATH a dugout in the original Support Trench at the end of the Medical Trench. Regimental Bearers bringing the first cases to Haywards Heath inform our squad there of the number of wounded to be brought in & the squad brings the wounded man & the message to BARTS & as many squads as necessary are then sent up beyond Haywards Heath to the Regimental aid posts. Evacuation is performed by relays of Bearers, viz: (1) aid posts to Barts' (2) Barts to Brewery. From the Brewery evacuation is by means of our own Motor Ambulances to the Dressing Station at ~~[illegible]~~ SAILLY LABOURSE. Where the three Tent subdivisions work, B & C at the School & A at the lightly wounded Dressing Station. All cases are completely redressed at SAILLY & inoculated against Tetanus & fed. Then evacuated by Motor Ambulance Convoy to BETHUNE or LILLERS.	

18

Instructions regarding War Diaries and Intelligence Summaries are contained in F. S. Regs., Part II. and the Staff Manual respectively. Title Pages will be prepared in manuscript.

Army Form C. 21[illegible]

WAR DIARY

or

INTELLIGENCE SUMMARY

(Erase heading not required.)

Imp. Hav., 26/7 — 10,000

Place	Date	Hour	Summary of Events and Information	Remarks and references to Appendices
1915 Sept	30th		The map appendix II shews the disposition of the advanced dressing stations	
			The classification of wounded admitted during September is as in the accompanying chart appendix I	
			Total admissions for August: Sick 421, Wounded 663, Gassed 2, 1086	
			Total since Feb 3rd: Sick 6251, Wounded 5882, Gassed 577, 12.710	

R. [illegible]
Lt Col
O.C. 85th (3rd London) Field Ambulance
28th Division

Appendix I.

CLASSIFICATION OF WOUNDED

Admitted to 85th (3rd London T) Field Ambulance – 1st to 30th September 1915

	Wounds of Head						Neck	Chest	Abdomen	Back-			Arms						Legs							Total No Deaths	Total No Wounds
	Scalp	Skull	Brain	Face	Jaw	Fract'd				Shoulders	Buttock	Back	Humerous	Fract'd	Forearm	Fract'd	Hand	Fingers	Thigh	Fract'd	Knee	Leg	Fract	Ankle	Foot		
Gunshot	10	9	1	23	3	(2)	3	17	7	23	9	10	26 1	(4)	55	(4)	40	25	20	-	8	20	(2)	3	8	1	320
Shrapnel	2	20	1	11	1	-	3	7	4	14	8	16	15 1	(3)	8	(1)	13	1	16	(1)	8	3	(2)	2	5	1	158
Grenade or Mortar	5	5	-	20			1	6	1 1	3	4	4	9	(2)	2	-	9	8	10	-	5	8	-	1	4	1	105
Bayonet																	1	1	1		1	1			1		6
Accidental		1	1														1	1									4
Totals	17	35	3	54	4	(2)	7	30	12 1	40	21	30	50 2	(9)	65	(5)	64	36	47	(1)	22	32	(4)	6	18	3	593

APPENDIX II

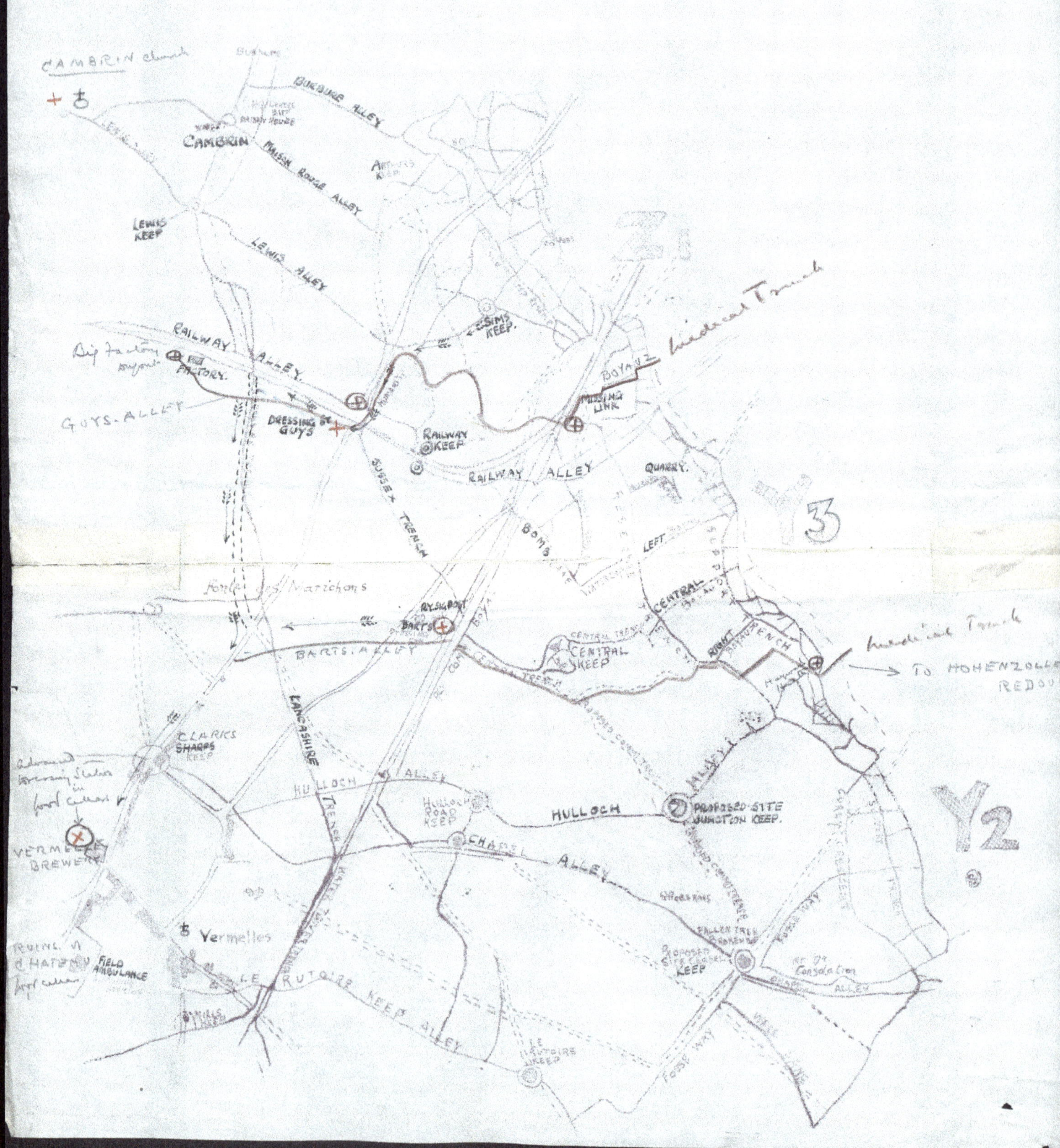

CAMBRIN church
CAMBRIN
BURBURE ALLEY
MAISON ROUGE ALLEY
ARTHURS KEEP
LEWIS KEEP
LEWIS ALLEY
RAILWAY ALLEY
SIMS KEEP
FACTORY
GUYS-ALLEY
DRESSING ST GUYS
RAILWAY KEEP
MISSING LINK
BOYAU 2
Medical Trench
SUSSEX TRENCH
QUARRY
BOMB
LEFT
CENTRAL
Y3
R.Y. SIG. POST
BART'S
BARTS ALLEY
CENTRAL KEEP
CENTRAL TRENCH
RIGHT
Medical Trench
TO HOHENZOLLE
REDOU
LANCASHIRE TRENCH
CLARKS
SHARPS KEEP
VERMELLES BREWERY
HULLOCH ALLEY
HULLOCH ROAD KEEP
HULLOCH
PROPOSED SITE JUNCTION KEEP
CHAPEL ALLEY
Y2
Vermelles
FIELD AMBULANCE
LE RUTOIRE KEEP ALLEY
LE RUTOIRE KEEP
PROPOSED SITE KEEP
FOSSE WAY

Oct 15

28th Division

121/7381

85th Field Ambulance

Vol X

Oct 15

Instructions regarding War Diaries and Intelligence Summaries are contained in F. S. Regs., Part II. and the Staff Manual respectively. Title Pages will be prepared in manuscript.

WAR DIARY
or
INTELLIGENCE SUMMARY
(Erase heading not required.)

Army Form C. 2118

Imp. Hay., 26/7 — 10.000

Place 1915	Date	Hour	Summary of Events and Information	Remarks and references to Appendices
Oct.	1st		Admitted Sick 42	
			Wounded 147 including x Capt. WRIGHT. T.N.T. 3/Yorkshire Regt attached 2nd	
			" WOOLLEDGE. J.G.P. RE. 95/Field Co	
			" LONGDEN. F.S. 2/Northumberland Fus.	
			2/Lieut SWEET. G.H.L. 2/ " "	
			2/ " GREW. B.D. 2/ " "	
			189 — 2/ " GATREW. R.J.M. 2/ E. Yorks.	
			Transferred to Clearing H. 183	
			Discharged to duty 5	
			Died 1 x	
	2nd		Admitted Sick 3 — including 2/Lieut CAMERON. F.S. 2/C...	
			Wounded 46 — 2/ " NEWINGTON. F. 2/E. Surreys attached 1/Welch	
			49	
			Transferred to Clearing H. 49	
			The Dressing Stations at SAILLY LABOURSE. Taken over by the 6th Field Ambulance 2nd Division at 9 am. & our Dressing Station & Head Quarters of unit with Transport Division removed to VENDIN near BETHUNE. Where we arrived at 1 pm. & B.S. Station opened up in the SCHOOL. Bearers continue VERMELLES.	
			Pte SPRATT. K.G. No 4558 wounded slightly by fragments of rifle bullet fired at the ground by a sick patient while cleaning his rifle.	
			Pte DUCKETT. & Pte DOBSON. J.W.S. rejoined off leave, having been detained by order of R.T.O. at Victoria in consequence of no boat being available on 29th.	

2/

Instructions regarding War Diaries and Intelligence Summaries are contained in F. S. Regs., Part II. and the Staff Manual respectively. Title Pages will be prepared in manuscript.

WAR DIARY
or
INTELLIGENCE SUMMARY
(Erase heading not required.)

Army Form C. 2118

Imp. Hav., 26/7 — 40,000

Place 1915	Date	Hour	Summary of Events and Information	Remarks and references to Appendices
Oct.	3rd		Admitted sick 3.	
			No wounded being admitted at VENDIN at present.	
			Capt: VICK. Capt: POTTER + 40 men from [illegible] Division relieved Capt: ROBBINS. CAPT: BARNSLEY + 35 men of Bearers at VERMELLES.	
			No 444 Pte BARNES. R + No 134 Pte KRANINGER. S proceeded on 5 days leave to England.	
	4th		Admitted sick 17	
			wounded 11 including Lt Col. HOGGAN. G.P. 1/[illegible] Rg. Lt Col. WHITE. F.A. 1/Suffolks.	
			28	
			Discharged to duty 1	
			Ordered to take in wounded at Dressing Station at VENDIN LEZ BETHUNE.	
	5th		Dressing Stations at VERMELLES taken over at 8pm by 9th Field Ambulance with the Guards Division. Our bearers at "Bart" & in outposts in central BOYAU TRENCH remaining there until the 84th Brigade were clear of the trenches & relieved by a Brigade of Guards, when they returned with Bearers from the Brewery to VENDIN. [illegible] to remain in billets at VENDIN until further orders & look after sick of Brigade.	

Instructions regarding War Diaries and Intelligence Summaries are contained in F. S. Regs., Part II. and the Staff Manual respectively. Title Pages will be prepared in manuscript.

3/

WAR DIARY
or
INTELLIGENCE SUMMARY
(Erase heading not required.)

Army Form C. 2118

Imp. Hav., 26/7 — 10,000

Place 1915	Date	Hour	Summary of Events and Information	Remarks and references to Appendices
Oct	5th		Admitted sick 26 / wounded 53 including Capt. HAWKESWORTH. J.L.J. 2/E. Yorks, 2/Lieut FRIER. N.E. 2/E. " — 79	
			Transferred to Cl[earin]g H 92 / Died 1	
	6th	3 am	Ordered to move 1 Tent Subdivision with 3 Horse ambulances with the 84th Brigade at 9 am & march with the Brigade to their new billeting area BERGUETTE – GUARBECQUE – BUSNES. via route CHOCQUES – BUSNES.	
		8.30 am	Tent subdivision of 'C' Section under Capt. VICK paraded & moved off with a motor cyclist to keep up communication. & took over billet at LA FLANDRE (CARNOT BOURDOIS)	
			Admitted sick 3	
			Discharged to Duty 1	
			Transferred to Cl[earin]g H 11	
	7th		'C' Section ordered to collect sick from the 84th Brigade & convey them to inspection room at their ('C' Section) billets & transfer them to head quarters of this unit at VERDIN by motor ambulances.	
			'B' Section at VERDIN. to take in the sick from the whole Division – (1). detain those likely to be fit for return to their unit in 2 days (2). send to a salvage company at divisional H.Q. BUSNES. those fit for light duty. (3) evacuate to Clearing H. all others	

Instructions regarding War Diaries and Intelligence Summaries are contained in F. S. Regs., Part II. and the Staff Manual respectively. Title Pages will be prepared in manuscript.

4

Army Form C. 2118

WAR DIARY
or
INTELLIGENCE SUMMARY
(Erase heading not required.)

Imp. Hav., 26/7 — 10,000

Place	Date	Hour	Summary of Events and Information	Remarks and references to Appendices
1915				
Oct. 7th			Captain BARNSLEY & Capt. K.V. SMITH with 95 N.C.O.s & men proceeded to join 'C' Section Tent Subdivision at LA FLANDRE in order to engage in Trench & Dug out digging & construction, under supervision of R.E.s & with the 84th Brigade & to undergo regular training whilst in billets.	
			The G.O.C. 1st Corps, 1st Army expressed his appreciation of the work the R.A.M.C. during the recent operations in front of VERMELLES & wished it to be placed on record.	
			Admitted Sick 23 Transferred to Clearing H. 9 Discharged to duty 1	
	8th		Sections employed at Physical & Company Drill, & checking & relocating equipment. All Kits, clothing &c inspected & overhauled & Transport vehicles & harness cleaned.	
			Pte PRATT. M.D. " ROSE. E.A. " SEVERN. A.E " STAFFORD. H } proceeded on leave to England till 13th inst.	
			Driver WILLIAMS. W.E. A.S.C awarded 4 days Field Punishment No. 1 for using insubordinate language to N.C.O. when rebuking him for being late on Roll Call.	

Army Form C. 2118

Instructions regarding War Diaries and Intelligence Summaries are contained in F. S. Regs., Part II. and the Staff Manual respectively. Title Pages will be prepared in manuscript.

5

WAR DIARY
or
INTELLIGENCE SUMMARY
(Erase heading not required.)

Imp. Hav., 26/7 — 10,000

Place	Date	Hour	Summary of Events and Information	Remarks and references to Appendices
1915 Oct	8th		Admitted Sick 36 including Major GEPP E.C. 3/A.E.L.I? Brigade Major 84th Brigade	
			Wounded 2	
			38	
			Transferred to Clearing H. 19	
			Discharged to Salvage Corp 15	
			" " Duty 5	
	9th		Admitted Sick 43	
			Wounded 2 – including 2/Lieut PEERS B. 2/KORL	
			45	
			Transferred to Clearing H. 15	
			Discharged to Salvage C. 5	
			" " Duty 2	
			All men not detailed for Hospital & camp duties employed in Physical drill, company & stretcher drill. Route marching & Trench digging daily while in this rest area.	
	10th		Unit inspected by D.D.M.S 1st Corps. 1st Army who expressed himself as pleased with all he saw.	

6

Instructions regarding War Diaries and Intelligence Summaries are contained in F. S. Regs., Part II. and the Staff Manual respectively. Title Pages will be prepared in manuscript.

WAR DIARY
or
INTELLIGENCE SUMMARY
(Erase heading not required.)

Army Form C. 2118

Imp. Hav., 26/7 — 10.000

Place 1915	Date	Hour	Summary of Events and Information	Remarks and references to Appendices
Oct.	10th		Admitted Sick 27	
			Wounded 3	
			30	
			Transferred to Clearing H. 13	
			Discharged to Salvage Co 6	
			" " Duty 6	
	11th		Admitted Sick 38	
			Transferred to Clearing H. 15	
			" ARGUES 1 — Eye case	
			Discharged to Salvage Comp 5	
			" " Duty 13	
			Several men occupied making Rope & network stretchers for carrying wounded through narrow & zig zag trenches.	
	12th		Admitted Sick 50 including Maj General BULFIN. E.S. G.O.C 28th Division	
			Wounded 1	
			51	
			Transferred to Clearing H. 23	
			Discharged to Salvage Co 8	
			" " Duty 7	

Army Form C. 2118

Instructions regarding War Diaries and Intelligence Summaries are contained in F. S. Regs., Part II. and the Staff Manual respectively. Title Pages will be prepared in manuscript.

WAR DIARY
or
INTELLIGENCE SUMMARY
(Erase heading not required.)

Imp. Hav., 26/7 — 10,000

Place 1915	Date	Hour	Summary of Events and Information	Remarks and references to Appendices
Oct.	13th		Admitted sick 42 wounded 4 46 Transferred to Clearing H. 27 Discharged to Salvage Co 5 " " to Duty 17 Sgt. RUSSELL. A.C. No 834 reported off leave	
	14th		No 182 Pte STEPHENS. P.M. officially awarded medal of St George 4th class for gallantry & distinguished conduct in the field, by H.M. the Emperor of Russia with approval of H.M. the King. No 98. Pte DOUCH. J.E. " 62. " JONES. H. " 479. " HETHERINGTON. F.W. " 313. " WELLER. H. } joined as reinforcements from the Base Admitted sick 43 wounded 3 46 Transferred to Clearing H. 3 Discharged to Salvage Co 14 " " Duty 7	

8

Instructions regarding War Diaries and Intelligence Summaries are contained in F. S. Regs., Part II. and the Staff Manual respectively. Title Pages will be prepared in manuscript.

WAR DIARY
or
INTELLIGENCE SUMMARY
(Erase heading not required.)

Army Form C. 2118

Imp. Hav., 26/7 – 10,000

Place 1915	Date	Hour	Summary of Events and Information	Remarks and references to Appendices
Oct	15th		Admitted Sick 60 including Lieut GODDING H.C. RAMC attached 2/KORL; 2/Lieut ESSEX A.C. 1/York & Lancs	
			Wounded 1	
			61	
			Transferred to Clearing H. 11	
			Discharged to Salvage Co 5	
			" Duty 7	
			No 148 Pte PRATT M.D., 267 " ROSE E.A., 96 " SEVERN A.E., 1123 " STAFFORD H } reported for duty off leave to England	
			Capt WOOTTON L.H. rejoined the unit from duty with 130th Howitzer Brigade RFA.	
	16th		Admitted Sick 48 including Lt Col SINCLAIR-THOMSON 1/Suffolk; Lieut CAYLEY C. 1/Monmouths; 2/Lieut O'BRIEN C.R. 2/KORL	
			Wounded 7 including 2/ " PLASKITT G.H. 10/Essex attached 1/KOYLI (Self inflicted)	
			55	
			Transferred to Clearing H. 27	
			Discharged to Salvage Co 16	
			" " Sanitary Sect 3	
			Discharged to Duty 12.	

Instructions regarding War Diaries and Intelligence Summaries are contained in F. S. Regs., Part II. and the Staff Manual respectively. Title Pages will be prepared in manuscript.

Army Form C. 2118

WAR DIARY
or
INTELLIGENCE SUMMARY
(Erase heading not required.)

Imp. Hav., 28/7 — 10,000

Place	Date	Hour	Summary of Events and Information	Remarks and references to Appendices
1915 Oct	16th	9 am	Orders to take over the ECOLE LIBRE des GARCONS on 18th from 22nd Field Ambulance as hospital & went over the premises with the O.C. Capt. WELLS. RAMC. & arranged time & method of the transfer.	
		10 am	Wire from 84th Brigade that they will march to LE QUESNOY on the morning of 18th inst.	
		4 pm	Went over to LA FLANDRE to see the Brigadier General. Lt Col WEIR as to starting point, time &c. & arranged to send 3 horse ambulances in rear of column to pick up stragglers & sick.	
		6.30 pm	Orders from ADMS to take over SCHOOLS at ANNEZIN at 9 am 17th from the 23rd Field Ambulance 7th Division	
		9 pm	Went to see O.C. Major BROWN. & inspected premises & arranged details of the transfer.	
		—	Sergt. UNDERHILL. F. reported off 1 month's leave to England on reengagement.	
			Pte BARNES R. reported off leave to England, which had been extended by A.G. War Office on account of urgent private affairs.	
		—	No 198 Pte DAVIS. M.P. & 167 " SPOONER. F.P. } proceeded to England to report to the "Directorate of Military Training" War Office, preparatory to a course of training for commissions in Regular Army.	
	17th	—	Capt. K.V. SMITH. detailed for & proceeded to duty with 28th Divisional Train HQ. till 31st inst.	
			No 283 Sergt. DORRINGTON. P. & 380 Sergt. GREENSLADE. F.C. } proceeded on 7 days leave to England.	

Instructions regarding War Diaries and Intelligence Summaries are contained in F. S. Regs., Part II. and the Staff Manual respectively. Title Pages will be prepared in manuscript.

10

WAR DIARY
or
INTELLIGENCE SUMMARY
(Erase heading not required.)

Army Form C. 2118

Imp. Hav., 26/7 — 10,000

Place	Date	Hour	Summary of Events and Information	Remarks and references to Appendices
1915 Oct	17th		~~Adm~~ "B" Section took over the Hospital at SCHOOLS. ANNEZIN & billets from the 23rd Field Ambulance at 9 am. Transferred 67 patients from our Hospital at VENDIN LES BETHUNE to ANNEZIN. B. Section Bearers rejoined the Section from LAFLANDRE (LE CORNET BOURDOIS) Admitted sick 30 including 2/Lieut CREE H.F. 2/E. Kents Transferred to Clearing H. 23 – including 1 dental case Discharged to Salvage Co 5 " " Duty 12	
	18th		Took over Hospital from 22nd Field Ambulance at 9 am. Advance party at 7.30 am. Transferred 14 cases from VENDIN to our new Hospital in BETHUNE. 'C' Section with A Section bearers marched with 84th Brigade from LAFLANDRE to BETHUNE & joined Head Quarters 1 mile at 1 pm. 'C' Section opened up & took over charge of Hospital. Admitted sick 17 including Lieut PETRE W. A.S.C. Transferred to Clearing H. 12 Discharged to Salvage Co 11 " " Sanitary Co 1 " " Duty 10	

Army Form C. 2118

Instructions regarding War Diaries and Intelligence Summaries are contained in F. S. Regs., Part II. and the Staff Manual respectively. Title Pages will be prepared in manuscript.

11

WAR DIARY
or
INTELLIGENCE SUMMARY
(Erase heading not required.)

Imp. Hav., 26/7 — 10,000

Place 1915	Date	Hour	Summary of Events and Information	Remarks and references to Appendices
Oct	18th	11 pm	Orders to hand over Hospital at BETHUNE to 86th Field Ambulance at ~~9~~ 12.30 pm. advance party from 86th to arrive at 9 a.m.	
	19th	12.30 pm	Packed up & marched out A & C Sections & handed over ECOLE LIBRE des GARCONS to 86th Field Ambulance. together with 14 lying cases.	
		1 pm	Joined up with B. Section at ANNEZIN.	
			Admitted sick 21 including 2/Lieut. JONES C.B. 2/North^d Fus	
			Transferred to Clearing H. 9	
			" 88th Field Amb 11	
			Discharged to [illegible] 5	
			" Duty 10	
	20th		Orders that 28th Division is leaving the 1st Army, & that this unit will be relieved by a Field Ambulance of 7th Division	1st Army
			Orders that this unit is to collect 7 Ford Sunbeam Motor Ambulances from the 47th Division & hand over our 7 Vauxhall Motor Ambulances in order that Motors of same types should be available within the area we are moving to.	1st Army
			Col HENVEY. A.A.Q.M.G. 28th Divn. agreed to our retaining our own Drivers.	
			Orders to exchange 21 H.D. Horses for 42 L.D. Horses & harness complete, & to hand over to Ordnance any surplus Ordnance Equip^t except Blankets & Stretchers, of which to carry as many as possible.	Corps
			Orders to replenish all Medical Equip^t at once, & to hand over any British Red Cross Society equipment to relieving Field Ambulance.	

12

Army Form C. 2118

Instructions regarding War Diaries and Intelligence Summaries are contained in F. S. Regs., Part II. and the Staff Manual respectively. Title Pages will be prepared in manuscript.

WAR DIARY
or
INTELLIGENCE SUMMARY
(Erase heading not required.)

Imp. Hav., 26/7 — 40.000

Place 1915	Date	Hour	Summary of Events and Information	Remarks and references to Appendices
Oct	20th		Orders to return to Divisional Train our 3 Bramble Limber wagons. to carry only 3 extra Bell Tents = 15 in all.	
			— All Ranks on leave recalled.	
			— Drew 42. L D in exchange for 21 H D Horses & Harness. 1 H D Horse died of [illegible]	
			Admitted Sick 19	
			Transferred to C Clearing Stn. 57	
			Discharged to duty 8	
	21st	12.30 am	— Orders to exchange (7) motor Ambulances with 47th Division at NEOUX LES MINES at 11 am.	}1st Army
			— Orders that 21st Division will entrain at FOUQUEREUIL & LILLERS starting at 12.35 am 21st completing at 6.57 24th. This unit to entrain at LILLERS at 2.57 am 24th — length of journey expected to be about 60 hours.	
		11 am	— completed the exchange of cars at NEOUX LES MINES. & sent 6 Wheel Ferguson attached 47th Division at MAZINGARBE, who agreed to the Drivers being retained with their original units.	
			Admitted Sick 4	
			Transferred to C Clearing Stn 8	
			" " Rest Station 2	
			Discharged to duty 7.	

Instructions regarding War Diaries and Intelligence Summaries are contained in F. S. Regs., Part II. and the Staff Manual respectively. Title Pages will be prepared in manuscript.

B

WAR DIARY
or
INTELLIGENCE SUMMARY
(Erase heading not required.)

Army Form C. 2118.

Imp. Hav. 26/7 — 10,000

Place	Date	Hour	Summary of Events and Information	Remarks and references to Appendices
1915 Oct. 22nd			Following men of A.S.C. joined as drivers of the 2nd L.D. horses drawn.	
			No. T/36222 Driver JONES. E. J. — 22nd Admitted Sick 2	
			" " CLEMENTS. J	
			" T/3.029134 " LINDLEY. W — Transferred to Clearing H. 5	
			" T/3.029918 " "	
			" T/3.023274 " ADKINS. C — Discharged to Duty 1	
			" T/. 32540. " DWYER. T — 23rd Admitted Sick 4	
			" T/3. 028376. " FERADAY. E — Transferred to Clearing H. 2	
			" T/4. 038166. " COOK. L — Discharged to Duty 12	
			" 891 " FREEMAN. C	
	23rd		All equipment was packed & loaded up by 12 noon. The unit marched at 8.15 pm 8 miles to LILLERS & entrained complete by 1 am. Train departed at 2.30 am. Stopped at intervals en route to enable men & horses to be fed & watered.	
	25th		Arrived at MARSEILLES at 11.20 am & marched to Camp in Parc BORELI & pitched Indian pattern Tents & marquees for personnel. Brought along several slightly sick men of 2nd Division in order to return them to units.	

Instructions regarding War Diaries and Intelligence Summaries are contained in F. S. Regs., Part II. and the Staff Manual respectively. Title Pages will be prepared in manuscript.

14

WAR DIARY

or

INTELLIGENCE SUMMARY

(Erase heading not required.)

Army Form C. 2118

Imp. Hav., 26/7 — 10,000

Place 1915	Date	Hour	Summary of Events and Information	Remarks and references to Appendices
Oct.	27th		Reported to A.D.M.S. Base (Colonel Hickson), who placed me in medical charge of Troops in the Camp. — Opened up a Detention Hospital in a building near the Grand Stand in the Park. 'B' Section opened.	
			Arranged with Capt. McEwen RAMC attached 21st Bgd RFA (who is appointed Sanitary Officer for the (camp) & Major R.G. [illegible] Base Sanitary Officer, details for improving present very defective system of camp Sanitation & water supply.	
	28th		In consultation with Genl. Arbuthnot, C.R.A. Camp Commandant & Sanitary Officers, arranged that camp should be divided up into areas for Sanitary control, under the Senior Officer with the units in each area, who will furnish all fatigue & police parties, under supervision of Sanitary Officers & Sanitary NCOs & be responsible for the duties being properly carried out.	
			— Route March & Bathing Parades for personnel.	
			Arranged with Col. Heneker A.A. Genl 28th Division to send the Field Ambulances complete in one Transport when embarking, & to detach 3 medical officers from each, to provide M.Os for the Transports conveying detachments & small units that have no M.Os.	

15

Instructions regarding War Diaries and Intelligence Summaries are contained in F. S. Regs., Part II. and the Staff Manual respectively. Title Pages will be prepared in manuscript.

Army Form C. 2118

WAR DIARY
or
INTELLIGENCE SUMMARY
(Erase heading not required.)

Imp. Hav., 26/7 — 10.000

Place	Date	Hour	Summary of Events and Information.	Remarks and references to Appendices
1915 Oct.	28th		The undermentioned were transferred sick to Casualty Clearing Station on 24th & struck off the strength of unit as from that date. No. 66 S/Sergt. BOYES. J.T. " 1556 Corpl. BAWTREE. A.L. " 362 Pte. CASWELL. F.T. " 1099 " FISHER. G.A.F. " 1094 " HALLS. E. " 293 " MICHIE. C.W.S. 27th Admitted Sick 15 28th Admitted Sick 17 including 2/Lieut. HAGGETT. H.F. ASC. 124th Supply Column [illegible] 22nd Div. Transferred to British [illegible] Lahore Indian Stationary Hospl. 4 Discharged to Duty 3 The undermentioned reported off leave at BOULOGNE on 20th inst. & rejoined the unit at MARSEILLES on 26th inst. No. 283 Sergt. DORRINGTON. P. " 380 " GREENSLADE. F.S. " 856 Corpl. YATES. E.	
	29th		The following officers were temporarily attached for duty as M.O.s while in the Camp Capt. POTTER. B.E. to 13th Heavy Battery & 31st Brigade R.F.A. " ROBBINS. H. to [illegible], Mobile Veterinary Section & other details " BARNSLEY. R.E. to 28th Division Regimental Transport " SMITH. K.V. to 28th " Ammunition Column	

Army Form C. 2118

Instructions regarding War Diaries and Intelligence Summaries are contained in F. S. Regs., Part II. and the Staff Manual respectively. Title Pages will be prepared in manuscript.

16

WAR DIARY
or
INTELLIGENCE SUMMARY
(Erase heading not required.)

Imp. Hav., 26/7 — 10.000

Place	Date	Hour	Summary of Events and Information	Remarks and references to Appendices
1915 Oct.	29th		Admitted Sick 15	
			Transferred to Lahore Indian Stationary Hospl. 2	
			Discharged to duty 5	
	30th		Admitted Sick 11	
			Transferred to Lahore Indian Stationary Hospl. 2	
			Discharged to duty 5	
		8.45 am	Orders from C.S.O. 28th Division to embark on "KARON" 124 men & 1 Officer of Field Ambulance as speedily as possible.	
		11 am	Lt. Col. W. S. Sharpe & 64 NCOs & men of 84th (2nd London) Field Ambulance & 60 NCOs & men of 86th (2/Northumbrian) Field Ambulance detailed & they left Camp at 11 am	
		8.30 pm	Orders from DA.QMG 28th Division to embark 40 men & 1 MO from the Field Ambulance soon as possible on the "KARON" detailed O.C. 86th Field Ambulance to embark 1 Officer & 40 men from his Field Ambulance at 11 pm.	
			Asked & obtained authority of ADMS MARSEILLES to use a large room at "Monnier" Halting establishment for accommodation of sick of the Division.	

17

Instructions regarding War Diaries and Intelligence Summaries are contained in F. S. Regs., Part II. and the Staff Manual respectively. Title Pages will be prepared in manuscript.

WAR DIARY
or
INTELLIGENCE SUMMARY
(Erase heading not required.)

Army Form C. 2118

Imp. Hav., 26/7 — 10,000

Place 1915	Date	Hour	Summary of Events and Information	Remarks and references to Appendices
Oct. 31st			Admitted Sick 4 Transferred to Lahore Indian Stationary Hosp^l 2 Discharged to duty 13. Sanitation of the Camp which was entirely neglected at the time of our arrival is now established on a satisfactory basis. Drinking water is provided from standpipes & led into 4 groups of 30 Barrels each. & sterilised by chlorination with bleaching powder. 15 in use & 15 in reserve in process of chlorination. Horses are watered from 4 - 75 metre lengths of trough, in place of 4 groups of tubs previously in use. 6. Latrines each of 50 to 70 "Buckets" have replaced short trench latrines. The Buckets are emptied into Tinnettes by Italian Labour & the latter removed & emptied twice a day by Contractors. Soak pits for urinals were hopeless as the soil did not permit soakage & have been replaced by Tinnettes which are emptied into the drains under the pavement of road. Incinerators have been built in each group of unit ground. & horse manure is dumped & carted by Contractors. Ablution places are in process of construction. Sanitary Squads & Police are provided by O.C.'s each area comprising the camps of 3 or 4 units. 6 areas are mapped out in the Camp. The health of the camp is good in spite of inclement weather.	

Army Form C. 2118

Instructions regarding War Diaries and Intelligence Summaries are contained in F. S. Regs., Part II. and the Staff Manual respectively. Title Pages will be prepared in manuscript.

18

WAR DIARY
or
INTELLIGENCE SUMMARY
(Erase heading not required.)

Imp. Hav., 26/7 — 10,000

Place	Date	Hour	Summary of Events and Information	Remarks and references to Appendices
1915			The classification of wounded admitted during October is as in the accompanying chart. appendix I Total admissions for October: Sick 666, wounded 280 — 946 Total since Feb 3rd: Sick 6917, wounded 6162, gassed 577 — 13,656 [illegible] Lt. Col. O.C. 85th (3rd London) Field Ambulance 28th Division	

APPENDIX. I

CLASSIFICATION OF WOUNDED

Admitted to 85th (3rd London T) Field Ambulance - 1st to 31st October 1915

	Wounds of Head						Neck	Chest	Abdomen	Back			Arms						Legs							Total No Deaths	Total No Wounds
	Scalp	Skull	Brain	Face	Jaw	(Fract')				Shoulders	Buttocks	Back	Humerus	(Fract'd)	Forearm	(Fract'd)	Hand	Fingers	Thigh	(Fract'd)	Knee	Leg	(Fract'd)	Ankle	Foot		
Gunshot	5	3	·	7			1	5	6 1	4	7	4	5 1	(2)	8		10	6	17	(4)	4	14	(2)	3	8	2	117
Shrapnel	3	5		7			1	2	1	2	8	4	6	(3)	6	(1)	3		6	(2)	2	7	(1)		3		66
Grenade or Mortar	1	1		7				1	1	1	3	2	4	(1)	4		6	2	4		2	7			2		48
Bayonet								1					1														2
Accidental		4		4						1			1				7	1	1		1	2					22
Shock effect of Shell explosion	–	–	–	–	–	–	–	–	–	–	–	–	–	–	–	–	–	–	–	–	–	–	–	–	–	–	25
	9	13	·	25	-	-	2	9	8 1	8	18	10	17 1	(6)	18	(1)	26	9	28	(6)	9	30	(3)	3	13	2	255

Total - 280

www.ingramcontent.com/pod-product-compliance
Lightning Source LLC
Chambersburg PA
CBHW081535160426
43191CB00011B/1762

* 9 7 8 1 4 7 4 5 2 4 6 2 9 *